# "PRESENT" YOURSELF IN PUBLIC SPEAKING

## TELL YOUR INNER CRITIC TO SHUT UP!
## AND THE REAL YOU TO SPEAK UP!

By
**Mary Cheyne**

# DOWNLOAD THE PRINTABLE
# COMPANION WORKBOOK FREE!

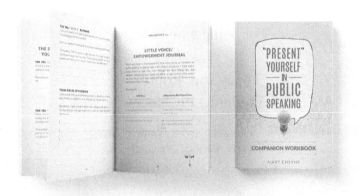

Just to say thank you for purchasing *"Present" Yourself in Public Speaking* I'd like to give you the *Companion Workbook* 100% free!

## CLICK·HERE·TO·DOWNLOAD¶
### HTTP://MAGNETICPODIUM.COM/PYIPS-WORKBOOK¶

# DEDICATION

To my husband and soulmate, Rob—
For being who you are

To my son, Robbie—
For being my teacher

To my niece, Natalie—
For inspiring me to write.

To my late mum Ame Y. Y.—
For your love and sacrifices

To my dad, Kim—
For setting the foundation

And last but not least, to you—
You are the reason I wrote this book.

# CONTENTS

# INTRODUCTION

You've probably heard that public speaking is people's number one fear, even before death itself. A 2014 *Washington Post* article, "America's Top Fears," reported, "The fear of public speaking is America's biggest phobia—25.3% say they fear speaking in front of a crowd." That's a large percentage, over one quarter.

Even celebrities have called attention to this "fear." Comedian Jerry Seinfeld commented, "That means to the average person, if you have to go to a funeral, you're better off in the casket than doing the eulogy."

So—where do you stand? Would you rather be in the casket than have to deliver the eulogy? Are you among the large group that considers public speaking their biggest fear? Do you know someone who is?

In my experience, people who think that public speaking is their big fear are actually a step away from their true fear. In reality, their number one fear is public *judgment.*

Think about it. The last time you had a presentation about which you felt a whole lot of nervousness and anxiety, wasn't it because, underneath it all, if you were totally honest with yourself, you were most fearful about what people were going to think about you? The bottom line—you wanted to look good and didn't want to look bad, right? Maybe you were concerned that you were going to be "found out" that you didn't really know what you were talking about or that your inadequacies would finally be revealed. Even people who consider themselves more advanced public speakers still have doubts in their heads, especially when speaking beyond their current comfort zone.

Do you know how I know this? Because, as public speakers, you and I share one thing in common. We are both humans. And as human beings, we have egos and pasts. And there lies the problem—how do we move beyond our egos and past conditioning to truly connect with the audience?

To catapult your public speaking experience, you need to be willing to take off your mask, look underneath it, and be actively engaged in looking at yourself. Then you can arrive at a new level of self-awareness, transforming yourself from the inside out. When you understand yourself, you will no longer just "survive" a presentation, but "thrive."

If you want to be completely uninhibited in front of an audience, express yourself freely, not be self-conscious, let your true, magnificent self shine through, and own your confidence, there needs to be nothing between you and the audience. You can connect with them because you are speaking from a place of full acceptance of who you are, imperfectly perfect, "warts 'n all."

In this book I'm going to show you how to do this through my specially developed inside-out approach. I've designed this book to be a roadmap to guide you on the journey to becoming a better speaker—from the inside out—as directly and as compassionately as I know how. I share processes that you can follow and practical and simple tools that you can use to get past each block that holds you back from having complete confidence as a public speaker and as a person—because these are inextricably linked.

There is a huge gap in public speaking education. From my observations, ninety-nine percent of public speaking books and courses only address mechanics in their effort to show participants how to improve their public speaking. And, yes, the mechanics of public speaking, meaning what you say (the content) and how you deliver it (the delivery) are very crucial in superb public speaking.

But—as you'll learn more fully in this book—the mechanics are only half the picture of public speaking. If anything, mechanics compose the most evident and easy-to-address elements in the public speaking improvement journey.

There is an entire other half that's rarely addressed, if at all, and definitely not to the level of depth that it needs because it is so important. And that's what I expose and guide you in understanding and improving in this book—the role of your psyche, your inside self, both cognitively and emotionally, that is at play in public speaking. Coming to terms with your inside—noticing, understanding, and working past these conscious and unconscious internal elements—is crucial in connecting with your audience and breaking through any fear and self-consciousness you may have.

It was only through my own journey of coming to know and work with my internal self that I was able to transform from a self-conscious computer programmer to competing in the 2009 World Championship of Public Speaking. I won second place out of 25,000 contestants from 14 countries.

I've now been a professional speaker and trainer for the better part of a decade.

After having tamed this fear of public judgment and self-consciousness—from the inside—I dissected the process in order to define it—what I'm calling the inside-out approach—to teach others who want to improve their public speaking abilities. Now, after having trained thousands of people and coached hundreds of individuals in public speaking, I know my inside-out approach works.

When I teach the tools and processes in the inside-out approach to students and coaching clients, I'm consistently met with uh-huhs and yeses along with the nodding of heads in agreement. They finally see past the veil that's been keeping them from showing their true, powerful selves to the audience. It's a big "aha" for them, and I know it will be for you as well, if you do the work.

From the thousands of people I've trained and the hundreds that I've coached, I saw patterns that emerged from every individual—blocks they had in common that they didn't even know they had. Blind spots within themselves that stood between them and their audience. These "blind spots" held them hostage from full self-expression and inhibited them from experiencing their own power on stage—and off.

You know that little voice of doubt in your head and the secret fear of what the audience will think? Now imagine having the presence of mind to snap yourself out of it. The inside-out approach guides you through the steps of how to do this, so you can become the best speaker you can be.

Being grounded in the understanding and armed with the tools and processes of the inside-out approach, you will never allow your critics (both internal and external) to ever stop you again. You won't be avoiding presentations like the plague, and you won't stress yourself out when preparing for a presentation you *have* to give. Instead of feeling self-conscious, you will be able to tap into the power that you have and didn't even know you had.

Cassie, one of my coaching clients, came to me from the professional world. Cassie works in marketing and communications, so she frequently has to deliver presentations to groups of people. She felt she was OK at it, but still she felt self-conscious.

After walking her through the inside-out approach, Cassie began to see that she unknowingly harbored a fear that was holding her back in public speaking. She realized that she feared people might think she was stupid. Through the process, she was able to determine exactly how that fear first entered her mind. Once she identified the source of the fear, she put aside that past baggage that she'd been unknowingly carrying on her shoulders for years. That fear was her barrier between her and her audience.

Cassie confided to me that now when she gives presentations and that old familiar fear of feeling stupid arises, she recognizes it and is able to let it go—on the spot—because she now knows that it's an illusion.

Shane, an expert in the finance field, gives trainings and presentations all the time. However, behind the scenes, he harbored the insecurity that he felt like a fraud. He felt that other people were more qualified than he was.

After I coached Shane through the inside-out approach, he realized that the biggest thing that stood between him and the audience was his own fear of not being good enough. Recognizing that was a light-bulb moment for him, and he now has the tools to reveal any disempowering illusions that he has about himself. Shane reported to me that now when giving presentations, his confidence level has increased considerably because he is now aware that he knows his material and is definitely not a fraud.

A college student, Yasmine, is a non-native English speaker and was timid and self-conscious about her accent and English. After following the inside-out approach and doing the work required, she became a powerful, inspiring motivational speaker in her own right. She now speaks regularly at various student organizations she belongs to, leads audiences in break-out sessions at conferences, and she even auditioned to become a group fitness instructor.

Yasmine has transformed into a different person than when I first met her. Now she's a woman who radiates warmth and confidence. And when the old self-doubts resurface, she has tools to snap herself out of it and put herself back into an empowering state.

This is the power of the inside-out approach. By doing the work of going through the inside-out roadmap, it transforms who you are as a speaker from within. I promise that if you are ready to break free from what's been holding you back in public speaking and if you read this book, follow the processes, and engage the courage to lift the veil of your "human-ness," then you will reclaim your own power. You'll not only "survive" a presentation—but THRIVE in public speaking. You will shine on the platform.

I will be honest with you—this inside-out approach of self-transformation can be confronting and, at times, even uncomfortable. But I promise, it will be worth it. Because waiting for you on the other side, is a confident, unstoppable you. And that confidence will translate to other areas of your life beyond public speaking.

Don't be the person who "already knows" all the "tips and tricks" there are about public speaking. I guarantee that by being open to the inside-out approach and really engaging with it, you will dive deeper into understanding and knowing yourself to break through to your best self.

Don't be the person who continues to sit on the sidelines while *other people* shine on the platform. Don't be the person who *survives* presentations or avoids them because *someone else* is better at it than you.

Be the person who acts in the face of doubt. Be the kind of person that, after speaking on stage, other people respond, saying, "You were so authentic. How do you do it?" Be the kind of person who takes action and does so—immediately. Not tomorrow. Not someday. *Now*—the time to act is now.

The golden nuggets you're about to read took me 15-plus years to develop. Over these years, I invested in self-education, training, many personal development courses and practices, and thousands of hours of experience, all of which allowed me to discover and connect the dots of what has been missing from public speaking teaching.

The inside-out approach I reveal in this book has already transformed the thousands of people whom I've trained. The light goes on in their eyes, and suddenly they have a different view of themselves. They understand themselves from a different perspective, and their experience of public speaking is never again the same. Why not experience this shift for yourself too?

All you have to do to experience the same shift is to keep reading. Each chapter will present new insights as you transform into the person and public speaker you've always wanted to be. To experience your true magnificence—from the inside-out—the time to take action is now.

# A PERSONAL NOTE

Dear Reader,

Let me start by saying—thank you for investing in yourself.

I'd like to share my story, so you know where I came from and why I wrote this book for you.

In one of my first jobs out of college, I was sitting in a conference room with 15 of my coworkers. After 45 minutes of people talking about systems and projects that I wasn't familiar with, the director turned to me and announced, "Mary, you're manager because Tim is out today. Why don't you give us an update on your team's projects?"

I froze. All I could see were eyes. All I heard was my own heart beating faster and faster. All I could feel was my face getting hotter and hotter. As this was happening I knew that this meant my face was getting redder and redder. It seemed like forever, until finally the director decided, "That's OK. Why don't we wait till Tim comes back next week."

Walking out of that meeting, I had never been so embarrassed in my entire life.

Six months later, I was sent to a conference with two co-workers from another team, Jack and Seth (nobody from my team wanted to go). A manager, Mindy, sat the three of us down to ask for our help. Mindy explained, "I'm working on initiating the Y2K project for our company. So while you're at the conference, can you talk to the other conference participants about what they've been doing at their respective companies about the Y2K issue?" I nodded in agreement.

However, at the conference, I was too self-conscious to talk to anybody, even individually. I just didn't have the self-confidence and was too socially awkward to approach anybody. I remember hating having this burden on my mind that I needed to talk to people.

Then, during a group session, I was in the audience with about 40 other people, and the facilitator brought up the Y2K issue. This was it, the perfect opportunity to naturally segue into the question I had so awkwardly tried to avoid asking. But, do you know what? I didn't raise my hand or say ANYTHING. I just sat there, like a stunned mullet, because I was too self-conscious, hoping that the information I needed would simply be fed to me.

A week later, back at the office I avoided Mindy like the plague. I reasoned with myself that Jack or Seth surely would have found the answers she needed already. My avoidance of Mindy was successful because she never followed up with me . . . I'm guessing Jack and Seth did do their homework (unlike me!).

I share this story to let you see where I came from. I was full of insecurity, self-doubt, and timidity (as hard as I tried to *fake* the opposite). I didn't even know I could be any different. I just knew I felt very self-conscious.

Maybe you have felt the same? That extreme avoidance of not wanting to speak in public, even in one-on-one situations, because you just don't know what to say or how to act around people.

I felt frustrated because I knew this self-consciousness didn't represent who I really was. I was hardworking and good at my job. I was smart and had personality and opinions. And around my close friends, I was fun. Why couldn't I just be my "real" self in public, in front of a group of people?

Maybe you've had the same frustration . . .

Believe me, I understand because I've been there and lived it, over and over again, until one day I declared, "Enough!" I didn't want to feel like this anymore. I was so sick of feeling self-conscious. I knew if there was ANY chance for me to progress in my career, I would need to DO something about it—and fast.

Fast-forward to August 2009: I stood on a stage in front of 2,000 people, competing in the finals of the World Championship of Public Speaking (did you know there was such a contest?). And out of 25,000 contestants from 14 countries, I came in second place.

Yes, you read that correctly—second place . . . Major shift from that fresh-out-of-college me, red-faced and choked by embarrassment when asked to speak in front of my work team!

Currently, I work as a professional speaker and trainer. I speak in front of people every day. At this point in my career, I have professionally trained over 15,000 people from 25 cities around the world. I can safely say that I'm very comfortable speaking in front of groups of people.

I tell these stories, so you know that you don't have to be BORN with the skill. Instead, what you need is a desire to become better, a willingness to engage in understanding yourself at a deeper level, and a solid work ethic.

Simply because you are reading this book, I believe you have all that. What you've been missing up to this point is guidance. And that's what this book will give you—an inside-out roadmap of the steps and processes that I wish I had when I began the journey of becoming a better public speaker. Much of the steps and processes in this book are ones I created for myself because no one was teaching what I needed the most—how to get out of my own way!

What you are about to read is a distillation of my many years of learning, so you can cut past your own "BS" and go straight through the eye of the needle—then you'll come out the other side being truly all that you were meant to be in public speaking, and in life: a communicator who is liberated in your expression and uninhibited by the audience. You have valuable messages to share with the world. Let the chapters of this book guide you to who you want to become.

And please remember: if I could do it, then I know anyone can. If I did it, then you can too.

I share the content of this book with you from the bottom of my heart. May you be your greatest self, the confident speaker. I know you can do it.

With much love and respect,

Mary

# PART I

## THE MISSING PIECES IN THE PUBLIC SPEAKING JIGSAW PUZZLE

# CHAPTER 1

# THE COMPLETE PUBLIC SPEAKING JIGSAW PUZZLE

I love this quote by one of my mentors, Adam Markel:

---

### THE DEFINITION OF A WARRIOR IS "ONE WHO CONQUERS ONESELF."

---

My intention is to guide you in gaining a greater understanding of yourself so that you can emerge on the other side empowered by your findings and never again be a victim of your fears.

The question is not *whether* you have these disempowering, unconscious thoughts; it's about your *having a process to conquer them* when they show up. As human beings, when we step outside of our comfort zone, those self-doubting thoughts will come up. Doing the work to see, face, and understand them so that they are no longer in your way is the key.

In essence, you're going to become a public speaking warrior who acts in spite of your fears and doubts. With my help you will break down misconceptions, lift the covers, look around the dark and sometimes scary corners, and access empowering perspectives—in order to allow the confident public speaker in you to emerge stronger than ever before.

Most public speaking assistance courses that exist, concentrate on the mechanics of public speaking. They stress voice, the structure of speech, how to stand, story-telling methods, eye contact, the deliberate use of pauses, etc. While all this is certainly a part of the public speaking experience, learning about it and practicing in these areas does not unlock the key to your public speaking dilemma—your own insecurities and self-doubts.

## The Revelation

One day early in my teaching of public speaking, a student came up to me after class and asked, "Mary, what else did you do besides speaking a lot to go from a self-conscious speaker to being so comfortable on stage that you do it for a living?"

In thinking about the answer and reflecting more deeply on my own journey, a revelation hit me like a ton of bricks: "I worked on myself." And you can do the same.

Let me explain what I mean by that.

## The Public Speaking Jigsaw Puzzle

And that's when I realized in the many, many public speaking trainings I'd attended, they only ever focused on HALF of the picture. Although they helped me tremendously in deconstructing my speeches and enhancing my delivery, that's still only half of the picture.

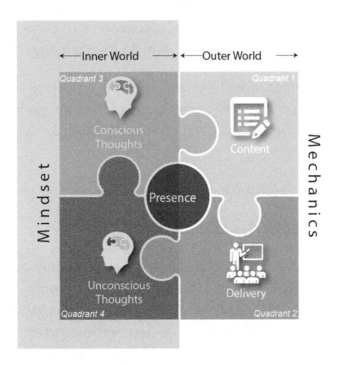

As you can see from the diagram above, the public speaking jigsaw puzzle is comprised of the following pieces:

**Content**—The first quadrant, *content*, is what you'll be speaking about: the message of your presentation, the stories and examples that you use, the points that you make, and the structure of your talk, which is how you weave all of this content together.

**Delivery**—The second quadrant, *delivery*, is you standing up in front of the room and presenting your content to a group of people. This includes eye contact, how you stand, your vocal variety (meaning your speech volume, rate, and pitch), your use of the stage, and maybe your use of props, gestures, and facial expression. These are all a part of delivery.

And this is where most public speaking education and trainings stop.

*The problem: content and delivery make up only half of the picture.*

As you'll see in the image above, content and delivery fall under the broad category of "mechanics," and that is only HALF of the public speaking jigsaw puzzle. There is an entire other half that's rarely addressed, if at all, and definitely not to the level of depth that it needs because it is so important.

**The Missing Half—Mindset**

There's an entire other half of the public speaking puzzle that I categorize under "mindset," which consists of your:

***Conscious thoughts***—Thoughts you're having and you're aware that they're there.

And more importantly:

*Unconscious thoughts*—Thoughts you're having that you don't even realize you're thinking.

In addition to mindset and mechanics, at the center of the public speaking puzzle is "presence." Bringing presence of mind to public speaking completes the public speaking puzzle. We will be talking extensively about stage "presence" in chapter 5. Right now, we're going to explore mindset in more depth.

## Mindset—Conscious and Unconscious Thoughts

I'm not saying that content and delivery are not important. They are very important and necessary. In fact, here are some resources that I recommend that specifically address content and delivery:

- Darren Lacroix's public speaking workshops: DarrenLaCroix.com
- Doug Stevenson's work on storytelling: www.Storytelling-in-Business.com
- Patricia Fripp's work on public speaking: www.Fripp.com
- Craig Valentine's work on public speaking and storytelling: www.CraigValentine.com
- Ed Tate's teachings on public speaking: EdTate.com

- These are all people I've learned from personally, and I have received a lot of value from their work.

What I *am* saying is that working on yourself by examining your mindset, both conscious and unconscious thoughts, including beliefs, is EQUALLY—if not MORE—important. When you work on yourself and know how to get out of your own way, that self-confidence transfers into all other areas of your life, not just public speaking.

Only one other speaker coach that I know of has made mention of this key to public speaking, Doug Stevenson, the Story Theater Method expert. His work also helped me along my journey. In a talk I heard him give at the National Speakers Association, he remarked that many public speakers lacked self-esteem and sought validation.

When I started teaching public speaking years ago, my experience supported Doug's observation. When I asked my students to name their biggest challenges when it came to public speaking, here are the answers I heard over and over again, from class to class, regardless of age, race, gender, and even experience level of the speaker:

- *I don't feel prepared enough.*
- *I feel nervous, especially if I don't feel prepared enough.*
- *In the Q and A section, I'm worried I'll get a question I don't know how to answer.*
- *I'm worried that the people in the audience know more than me, like if my superiors are in the room.*
- *I get nervous and I go blank.*

As I took them through the inside-out approach that you are embarking on, I gently encouraged them to dig a little below the surface to see what hid behind these concerns. And what hid behind the initial conscious concerns were their unconscious thoughts.

The majority of thoughts that stand between you and the audience are unconscious ones, things you think but don't even realize you are thinking. They are blind spots. For example, concerns like "I don't feel prepared enough" belong in the realm of conscious thought. Why? Because this is a thought that you know you are having.

The unconscious thought hidden below the surface might be "I'm not good enough" or "I'm not qualified enough, and they will find out." When these thoughts remain hidden, they feel real, like the "truth," so you act and behave within the boundary of this "truth." Hence, the anxiety and nervousness you feel.

It's not just you. It might help you to know that *everyone* has thoughts that are "hidden" from their immediate view.

Again—it's *not* just you. Even the most confident person you know experiences these thoughts, especially when that person is outside of their comfort zone.

Do you know how I know? Because we are all human! And all human beings have fears, doubts, and insecurities.

## Internal World vs. External World

If you draw a vertical line down the middle of the public speaking jigsaw puzzle, the right side is the "outer world," consisting of content and delivery, things the audience can see, hear, feel, and maybe even touch, if props are used during a presentation.

The left side of the puzzle is the "inner world," what is transparent to the audience but real for the speaker. This is what goes on inside the speaker's mind. Your thoughts can appear as real to you as a physical object placed in front of your face.

Although no one else outside of you can see or hear your thoughts, your internal world is JUST as important as the external one. In fact, arguably even more important because it is your interpretation within your internal world that largely determines your experience of the outer world.

## Hardware vs. Software

I started my career in the technology world, and it's still a technology-driven world, even more so. Even my 82-year-old grandmother-in-law uses an iPad mini. So let's use technology as an analogy:

Let's say you print out a page of words, and it looks wrong. There are spelling errors, grammar mistakes, and an image that's in the upper right corner instead of the bottom left corner like you wanted. So what do you do? What if you were to turn the printer off, then back on, and reprint the page? Well, it comes out the same way, doesn't it?

So, now you're a little annoyed. You press buttons on the printer—still the same result. OK, now you've had it, you don't have the patience, so you get a hammer, and beat the printer up.

No! Of course not! That won't solve the problem—but what would?

You go to the writing application on your computer, such as Microsoft Word, and fix the problem there. You use the writing software to help you—spell check, grammar check, and repositioning of the image on the page.

It sounds obvious, right? Of course!

I use this analogy because what most people do when they try to improve their speeches is deal with the machine only. They press the buttons on the printer—the delivery—and change out the paper—the content—when really what they ought to focus on is changing the software itself—their mindset.

You have to look at yourself holistically. And that's what I'm teaching you in this inside-out approach: examining the internal world of public speaking, public speakers themselves, i.e., you.

## Barriers between You and the Audience

### *Physical Barrier*

I'm going to use physical barriers to public speaking as a comparison. You'll see exactly how it's relevant to what we're talking about in just a few minutes.

If there's a lectern available on stage, most speakers will stand behind it. It's the norm. However, I coach my students and speaking clients to avoid standing behind the lectern. Instead, stand in the middle of the stage where there is no physical barrier between you and the audience.

I notice many people like to use the lectern to rest their elbows on or to have somewhere to put their notes. Behind the lectern is where they can "hide" and feel safe. They don't like to "stand out" of the crowd. Here's some news you may not want to hear: if you are speaking in front of a group of people, you are already standing out from the crowd, so you might as well embrace it and go whole hog. Why not?

That zone of safety is a crutch. Yes, most people stand behind the lectern. But most people don't know any better. The lectern is literally a physical barrier between you and the audience. You really can't argue with that.

If you do have notes, make them simple and in big font, and place them on the floor in front of you on the stage. That's what I do. You'll need to arrive early and place them there before the event begins. If you feel that's too weird, you can carry notecards.

### *Mental and Emotional Barriers*

While it's easy to see and understand a physical

barrier between you and the audience, it's not as easy to see mental and emotional barriers that exist between you and the audience.

You can have all the right mechanics, but if you don't address your software, i.e., your thought processes and mind, there may be mental and emotional barriers between you and your audience that you don't realize are there.

Let's take a closer look at this. If I was able to zoom into your head while you were speaking in front of an audience and listen to what was going on in there, it might go something like this:

- *I'm so nervous.*
- *Am I making any sense?*
- *Am I being engaging?*
- *What will they think of me?*
- *What if they hate what I'm saying?*
- *What if they ask me a question I don't know?*
- *I feel so awkward.*
- *I just sounded so stupid.*
- *I feel like an idiot up here.*

Does this sound familiar?

How can you connect with ANYONE if you have all of that NOISE in your head? How can you focus on your audience when you can't get past yourself?

In all of those thoughts, who was the focus on? *Me, me, me, me, me.*

Let me ask you a question: how the heck can you focus on the audience if your focus is on yourself, your own doubts, your own insecurities, your own LITTLE VOICE?

The answer is, you can't! UNLESS you:

- Recognize that the little voice in your head exists.
  —And—

- Know how to get over it so that it no longer becomes a distraction that weighs on your self-confidence.

And that's what we'll dive into in chapter 2, Lifting the Veil—Why You ACTUALLY Get Nervous.

## Value Progress

If you want to become a better public speaker, you have to put progress right up there on your list of values.

And, you need to ask yourself one question and

answer it very honestly: *What am I about? Am I about PROGRESS or PLAYING IT SAFE and LOOKING GOOD?*

If you value PROGRESS, then you put yourself on the path to personal mastery. I believe that you value progress because you're reading this book. You want to bring out the best speaker in yourself.

Dr. Michael Gervais, a high performance psychologist and recognized speaker on optimal human performance, who has worked with top athletes, musicians, artists, Olympic gold medalists, and the NFL Seattle Seahawks says:

---

## "PERSONAL MASTERY" IS ABOUT MASTERY OF SELF AND THE CRAFT.

---

This quote wraps up what chapter 1 has been about—to master the craft of public speaking, it's not just about mastering the craft (think—content and delivery); it's also about mastering yourself (think—your mindset, the world of conscious and unconscious thoughts).

We will further address the path of mastery in chapter 6, The Process of Mastery.

## CHAPTER 1 GOLDEN NUGGETS

To become a better public speaker and overcome the fear of public speaking, it's not enough just to work on the mechanics of public speaking. Although the mechanics of content and delivery are necessary and important, it doesn't address the whole picture. To liberate yourself from the prison of fear and anxiety about speaking in front of a group of people, you must also, just as importantly, do the following:

- *Work on yourself.* You are the common denominator. When you work on yourself and achieve insights and breakthroughs, your increase in confidence will "bleed" into your public speaking experience and into other areas of your life.

- *Muster the courage to examine your unconscious thoughts* that are hiding behind your conscious concerns. Because it's the thoughts you don't even realize you have that hold you back, putting up an invisible wall between you and the audience.

- *Value progress.* Rather than attaching false hopes to being an excellent public speaker overnight and then beating yourself up when reality doesn't match that expectation, you need to pat yourself on the back for the progress you make each time you get up and speak, and each time you put in the effort that I'm asking of you as you pursue the inside-out approach.

- *View yourself as a public speaking warrior—one who conquers yourself.* Only when you understand yourself can you transcend your doubts and insecurities and act in spite of fear, changing the focus from you to those whom you're there to serve—your audience.

# PART II

## LOCATING THE MISSING PIECES

# CHAPTER 2

# LIFTING THE VEIL—WHY YOU ACTUALLY GET NERVOUS

What most of us don't realize is we each have an inner critic. And when it "speaks" to us, that little voice comes from fear—our survival instinct. We, as humans, are hardwired to survive, so the little voice tries to convince us to stay within our comfort zone. Why? Because outside our comfort zone it might be dangerous, and we may not survive.

The first step: become aware that you have a constant communicator, an inner critic, in your head.

Knowing both why it's there and how the human fear of social rejection sits between you and the audience will help you understand why you get nervous speaking in front of a crowd.

Public speaking is about a human connection with the audience. If you are "messed up" or mixed up inside, with chaotic thoughts and emotions that stem from the fears mentioned above, then you are not clear and available to connect with your audience. You are too distracted.

In this chapter, we're going to hold a looking glass on ourselves as human beings and examine the origins and manifestations of this fear and nervousness around public speaking.

## What They Don't Tell You

Unfortunately, we're not taught how to deal with ourselves, meaning how to process our thoughts and emotions, so we can empower ourselves. In fact, there are many important life skills that school did not teach us. Robert Kyosaki, author of *Rich Dad Poor Dad*, points out that money management is not taught in school. And he is right. And neither is communication and how to deal with emotions, both of which I discovered are very closely related.

School focuses on hard skills, like math and science. There isn't a lot of focus on understanding human psychology or understanding ourselves—how we, as humans, process our thoughts and emotions, and, more importantly, how to do so in ways that empower us.

And what has knowing how to process your thoughts and emotions got to do with public speaking? Everything!

Public speaking is a human being (you), relating to and connecting with other human beings (your audience). And how can people relate deeply to one another? Yes, you exchange information (content). Yes, good speeches have take-away messages.

But the great speeches are the ones that affect people on an emotional level. In order to move your audience on an emotional level, then you must first know yourself on a deep emotional level.

Let me add too that the skill and process of knowing how to process your thoughts and emotions in an empowering way are rarely taught in families. I certainly did not learn it from my parents.

## Internal Critic

I'm now going to lead you through some steps that will help you to understand yourself better and become a better public speaker:

## Step 1—Know Your Strengths

If I were to ask, "What are your top three strengths when it comes to public speaking?," what would you say? In my workshops, most people don't have too much trouble coming up with three (we will return to this in more detail in chapter 3).

Now if I were to ask you to write out your 52 strengths, what would your reaction be? Perhaps you'd ask, "Why 52?" Because I call this your "Deck of Strengths," like how a deck of playing cards has 52 cards.

In my workshops, I give participants three minutes to write down as many of their strengths as possible. No one has managed yet to name all 52 within that timeframe. The common number is somewhere between 10 and 30.

You can find the *Deck of Strengths Exercise* as *Worksheet #2* in the *"Present" Yourself in Public Speaking Companion Workbook*. (If you've not yet downloaded the workbook, please go here to download it now http://magneticpodium.com/pyips -workbook, so you can use this handy tool immediately!) Spend three minutes filling it out, and only write one strength in each box. Also, these strengths don't have to be related to public speaking. For instance, the following are examples:

friendly, open, humorous, hardworking, honest, optimistic.

WAIT! Before you dive into this exercise, read step 2 below:

## Step 2—Notice What Comes Up

As you write these 52 strengths, I'd like you to pay attention to what comes up in your mind AS you're doing this exercise. Pay attention to any thoughts, feelings, impulses, reactions—basically ANYthing that comes up that you notice while you are writing your strengths.

There is no right or wrong here. It's a matter of noticing that inner voice as you are doing the writing for this activity. The more honest you can be with yourself, the faster you will progress in the process of mastering yourself from the inside and public speaking.

Now, you are ready to dive into the Deck of Strengths Exercise. And don't forget to notice what else comes up as you do it!

## Debrief on Deck of Strengths Exercise

In my workshops, after participants have done the Deck of Strengths Exercise, they then take a moment to write out what they noticed coming up for them internally during the exercise. When participants share what they noticed, some common themes emerge. Here are the most common:

- *I thought about how I was at work versus at home.*
- *I thought about what my family and friends have said about me.*
- *I felt like I was boasting.*
- *I kept thinking about my weaknesses.*
- *A strength would come to mind, like "I'm courageous," and then I would think, "Well, I am in some situations, but I'm not in other situations, should I write that down then if I'm not like that in ALL situations?"*

## What's the Connection to Public Speaking?

There are two main ways that this is connected to public speaking:

1. In my years of experience teaching public speaking, I noticed that for most people, when they are on the platform speaking, they're not thinking about their strengths. Guess what they're thinking about? You guessed it—their weaknesses.
2. When you're in front of a group speaking, there are TWO voices happening at the same

time: the one coming out of your mouth AND the one that's going on in your head.

## Your Little Voice

I'd now like to introduce you to someone who you've known for a very long time, only you may not realize that they even exist. Yes. I'd like to introduce you to your little voice.

In my workshops I lead participants through exactly the same process as you just read—and hopefully just did. Right after I say, "I'd like to introduce you to your little voice," I leave them in silence for about 30 seconds and just look at them. Curiosity turns into weird looks, first at me and then at each other. More silence. At this point they usually burst into giggles.

I continue, "If you're hearing, 'What is she talking about? What little voice? Is she crazy? This is weird . . .' THAT'S THE LITTLE VOICE!"

I'm talking about the little voice that always talks to you in your head—commenting, judging, saying something to you. Only once you are before an audience, it gets that much louder. For example, have you ever been speaking in front of a group and the little voice in your head comments, "Oh my god, what you just said was so stupid!"?

When I ask my class this same question, the most common response is that they burst out into giggles or full laughter in unison. They're not laughing AT me; they're laughing WITH me because they know EXACTLY what I mean.

## Why Do We Need to Talk about the Little Voice?

To be the best speaker you can be, you need to be present with the audience (something we'll address more in chapter 5, Presence). However, if you are listening to your little voice like it is accurate, then it will derail you from being present with the audience, every time.

In my classes, I'll ask for a volunteer to come up to the front of the class. My request is typically met with hesitant silence.

I'll then say, "Pause right there! What's your little voice saying right now?"

At this point, I'm again usually met with giggles.

"Is your little voice saying to you, 'Someone else can do it better than you can. You don't want to look stupid'? You don't have to tell me; just notice what it's saying and notice how you're buying into what it's saying and how it stops you from taking action."

In the next section we will look at the little voice directly and recognize it for what it is, so it will no longer be the driver of your decisions.

## Common Little Voices

In my training of thousands of people and coaching of hundreds, I typically hear the same concerns. Essentially, I noticed that ALL of people's individual little voices are saying similar things. Here are the most common utterings of people's little voices. Can you identify with them?

- *I don't want to look stupid.*
- *I don't like being in front of a room.*
- *I'm so nervous and feel a lot of anxiety when public speaking.*
- *I'm good with a small group but lose it with a big group.*
- *I'm anxious when I think that the people in the audience know more than I do about the topic I'm speaking on.*
- *I hate the "Questions and Answers" section. I fear that I'll get asked a question I don't know.*
- *I want to be relaxed and not take myself so seriously up here—but I can't.*
- *I'm afraid of messing up and embarrassing myself.*

- *I feel like I am a fraud (imposter syndrome).*
- *I have a message/story to tell, but I don't have the confidence.*

## A Personal Example

One of my re-occurring disempowering little voices is "You should know that." And when this little voice came up, it used to debilitate me from asking questions.

And why was that debilitating? Because the fear of public judgment was present. The little voice was trying to "save" me from looking stupid.

I've been aware of this little voice for quite some time, so now when it comes up, I catch it really quickly, so it doesn't stop me from asking my question. I've learned to recognize it and nip it in the bud.

For example, recently I attended a conference. The presenter was talking about global warming. During her speech, when she noted, "Students in the United States are taught very differently than in Asian countries," this piqued my interest. I wondered what she meant by that.

At the end of her talk, when she asked, "Are there any questions?" a few people raised their hands and asked questions related to global warming. I wanted to ask my question, but I was aware of what my little voices were telling me, "You're Asian, so you should already know how students in Asian countries are taught. Everyone else is asking about global warming. What's your question got to do with global warming?"

So what did I do? I'll tell you in the section, "Antidote to the Little Voice." Also, in chapter 3, Empowering Yourself, we explore more deeply where these little voices come from and how to debunk them at the source.

For now, remember—to become confident in speaking in public, you need to practice noticing the voices as they are happening in real time. As with any skill, this will initially be challenging to do because they happen so fast—and that's why it takes practice.

## Inner Critic—Yours Is Not the Only One

The disempowering little voices are what your inner critic is saying to you. I assure you that you are not the ONLY one who has an inner critic—although it can FEEL like it because the inner critic keeps you feeling like a hostage of your fears, insecurities, and self-doubts by constantly whispering into your ears.

Most of the time the whispers happen so fast that all you detect is an eerie, gut-wrenching fear disguised as "the truth." For example, if in the middle of your speech, you hear your inner critic saying the words, "You suck," how does that make you feel?

Here are some people you may know who have talked about their inner critics:

Amy Poehler, the award-winning actress from the television show *Saturday Night Live,* in her hilarious autobiographical book, *Yes Please*, calls her inner critic the "demon." She describes it like this: "That voice that talks badly to you is a demon voice . . . It tells you that you are fat and ugly and you don't deserve love. And the scary part is the demon is your own voice."

Julia Cameron, creativity teacher and author of the international bestselling book *The Artist's Way*, says that she discovered that many of her students were blocked creatively because of their "monsters," often a past authority figure, such as a parent or teacher, who spoke negatively of their creative efforts. And the negative comments from the past "scarred" them and got embedded in their sub-conscious, so they adopted it as their own in the form of the inner critic.

Dr Brené Brown, research faculty member at the University of Houston and author of the bestselling books *The Gifts of Imperfection* and *I Thought It Was Just Me*, calls the inner critic "gremlins." If you are too young to remember, there was a famous movie in the 1980s called *Gremlins*. Gremlins were nasty, little creatures that caused trouble and wreaked havoc throughout the town.

Dr. Richard Carson, practicing psychotherapist of over 35 years, wrote an entire book on the issue: *Taming Your Gremlins*. He founded the Gremlin Taming Institute that trains mental health professionals, corporate executives, and substance abuse specialists.

Judy Carter, comedian and author of *Stand-up Comedy: The Book*, simply calls it your "critic." Judy educates and entertains by recommending, "Take your critic out for a walk . . . Give your critical voice a real name . . . Write down everything it says like a court reporter . . . Write your response. Dialogue with the bully."

Coincidentally enough I did give my own inner critic a name. My World Championship speech was about my inner critic, and I personified her and called her "Nelly," based on the character Nelly from *The Little House on the Prairie* TV series. Nelly was a girl bully who would make the main character, Laura Ingle's school life hell.

Tara Mohr, author of *Playing Big—Find Your Voice, Your Mission, Your Message*, is an expert on women's leadership and well-being. In coaching her clients, many of whom were talented professionals, she noticed that they were letting their inner critics stop them from playing big in their lives and careers.

In *Playing Big* Mohr lists various qualities of the inner critic, with my favorite being: *if it's something you wouldn't say to your best friend, then it's your inner critic*. I love this so much so that in my classes I started something that I call the "Best Friend Test." Here's how it works: if that little voice in your head is saying something that you would not say to your best friend, then why would you want to say it to yourself?

My very first mentor in public speaking, Terry Viney, used to say to me, "Mary, if we talked to our friends the way we talk to ourselves, we wouldn't have any friends." He was talking about the little voices of our inner critics.

## Why Debunk Your Inner Critic?

It's important to pay attention to your internal dialogue because what you say to yourself affects your physiology and can stop you from doing what's in your best interest—this not only applies to your public speaking aspirations but to your potential to live the best life possible.

Thoughts lead to feelings. And feelings are chemical reactions within the body felt as an emotion. And your body reacts to what you say to yourself. I first saw this in a Jack Canfield's "Success Principles" demonstration.

In the demonstration Jack called a volunteer from the audience to the front of the room. Let's call her Susan. He asked Susan to raise her right arm out straight and say, "My name is Linda," (a fake name). While she said this, Jack tried to press her arm down and was able to do so.

Jack then asked Susan to say the truth, "My name is Susan." And again, as she said the sentence, Jack tried to press her arm down. But, this time he was not able to. The point: when you are saying something that is not true to who you really are, your body reacts differently.

It's in your best interest to watch what you are saying to yourself because it clearly affects how you feel and even how your body reacts. You want to feed your mind and, as a result, your body, only nutritious thoughts that empower you. Also, you must know how to recognize and then debunk the thoughts that are disempowering.

**The good news**—you'll be pleased to know that there IS an antidote to these disempowering little voices.

### Antidote to the Little Voice

The antidote to the disempowering little voices is very simple: two words, both beginning with the letter A:

---

## AWARENESS AND ACTION

---

Like I said, it's very simple. But simple does not mean it's easy. There is a difference.

Losing weight is very simple—eat less (or a lot less) and exercise more. But is it easy? In many cases, no. It's a habit you need to build. It takes time, focused intention, and repeated effort, especially after setbacks, to make something a habit.

While you are on the platform, when things are happening in real time, it is extremely tricky to "catch" those disempowering little voices as they are happening. But this is exactly what I'm asking you to practice.

I have an exercise in my classes in which I have each student speak and then immediately afterwards we debrief in front of the class, with me asking, "Could you hear the little voice? What was it saying?" I recommend asking yourself these two questions immediately after a presentation or speech. The more honest you are with yourself, the faster you will gain awareness and the faster you will improve.

It's almost like catching wind—that's impossible. So "catching" is not the most accurate action. It's more like "noticing," noticing the little voice and allowing it space to pass by.

For example, remember my little voice, "You should know that," that came up during the question and answer period at the end of the presentation about global warming? Here's what I did when I heard my "Don't ask the question, you should already know that" voice: I noticed the little voice AND asked ANYWAY.

Do you see that had I not have been practiced and aware enough to notice the little "You should know that" voice, then I would have dutifully listened to it, activating my human fear of judgment, and then it would have stopped me from asking the question I wanted to ask?

That's how the little voice stops you from speaking up: by appealing to your fears, the fear of being judged in this case.

There are other little voices too that stem from different human needs as we'll discuss later in this chapter.

## Parrying the Punches

In karate, there is a technique called "parry." When an opponent extends a punch at you, as their fist is traveling towards you, you see it coming and use the palm of your hand to simply "guide" it away from the center of your body (your centerline). In this way the punch will travel past your body, so you don't directly take its full impact.

You can apply the same technique to those little voices in their attempts to ambush you—think of it as a "mental" parry within your own head. For example, imagine you are up on the platform, speaking to an audience right now, and you notice the little voice talking to you:

**Little Voice**: What you just said was stupid.

**You**: I'm aware of what you just said [*parry it off to the side*].

**Little Voice**: They're gonna know you're a fraud.

**You**: I'm aware of what you just said [*parry it off to the side*].

**Little Voice**: The guy in the back row looks bored. You must be boring.

**You**: I'm aware of what you just said [*parry it off to the side*].

Later in chapter 3, Empowering Yourself, we will talk about the source of the disempowering little voices, limiting self-beliefs, and a process called the 3Rs that you can use to nip the little voices in the bud in your own time, not just when you are "live" on stage.

**Stop. Reset. Continue**

In my World Championship speech, I talked about the inner critic: that voice in your head that tells you you're not good enough. In the seven minutes that I had, I gave the audience a high-level solution to get past their inner critic:

*Stop*: and notice it

*Reset*: come back to presence

*Continue*: to take action.

That's how I handle my inner critic.

## Non-Native English Speakers—Extra Little Voices

Imagine I asked you to give a presentation in a language that you're learning, say German (and German is not your native language). The people in the audience are native German speakers. Would you feel self-conscious? What little voices (on top of the regular ones) do you imagine you would hear? That's what non-native English speakers deal with when giving presentations in English.

I interviewed Dr. Christi Barb, an accent modification expert. She shared that the following are the common little voices non-native English speakers might hear:

- *People are judging my intelligence by the way I speak. They'll think I'm incompetent because my English is not good enough/perfect.*

- *I feel self-conscious making those sounds with my mouth that I'm not used to making.*
- *I didn't pronounce that right; therefore, I didn't communicate well.*
- *It takes me way too long to think of the right English word.*
- *I feel like putting on an American accent feels fake, and I'm just pretending to be somebody I'm not.*
- *My friends will ask me why I'm speaking like an American and if I am ashamed of being Spanish/Chinese/Indian/etc.*

## Advice for Non-Native English Speakers

Here is some advice from Dr. Barb specifically for non-native English speakers who are giving presentations or speaking in public using English:

1. Confidence comes from being comfortable with being uncomfortable.
2. Start small and take baby steps.
3. Focus on your long-term goal.
4. Accent modification is not about "fixing" the way you speak. It's about giving you more options to choose from.

To find out more about Dr. Barb's work and how she can help you as a non-native English speaker, go to her website http://www.adastraspeech.com/

## Origin of the Inner Critic

In order to release ourselves from the hold that the inner critic has over us, we need to first understand the nature of the inner critic. Why is it there? Why does the inner critic exist? What is its purpose? In understanding the inner critic's nature and origin, it becomes easier to identify the disempowering voices as they come up, when they do. Once we hear them, we don't need to let them stop us.

But first we need to recognize it for what it is. Let's dive in.

## Past Conditioning

I used to be a programmer. The way our minds are "programmed" is analogous to the way a computer is programmed. We, as humans, get "programmed" as well. Events and interpretations of those events that happened to us in the past get programmed into our brains.

For example, you touched fire. You felt pain. A new program was installed in you:

## FIRE = HOT! DON'T TOUCH.

This is a simple example. There are many others. Not all of them are conscious. In fact, many of them are unconscious, designed to keep you safe and away from pain.

**Seeking Approval**

So, over and over again, we were conditioned as children to seek our parents', teachers', and caretakers' approval. And when we did do something that did not meet their approval, we usually got into trouble after they found out about it.

For example, when I was 9 years old, my mum forbid me to ride my bike after dark. One night, I snuck out and went on a bike ride. When she found out, she confiscated my bike and smacked me hard. The lesson that was programmed into me was "Don't break the rules. If I do, I will experience pain, the wrath of Mum."

Here is another example. In the third grade, I was talking to my friend in class while my teacher, Mrs. R, with her long silver hair tied into a tight bun, was trying to explain something. I heard, "Young lady, what did I just say?" When I couldn't repeat it, with a stern look on her face Mrs. R remarked, "That's because you were talking!" Lesson learned: talking = bad.

As youngsters, we rely on our parents and caretakers to keep us alive. As babies we are defenseless, completely dependent beings. We need our parents to feed us, dress us, bathe us, and keep us safe. We need their love, support, and actions to live. So, unconsciously, we are conditioned to seek their approval. If we lose their approval, we might get into trouble and get yelled at or smacked, both unpleasant, both painful. And at the worst end of the scale, we might be abandoned, so we no longer have a means of survival.

## We Never Heard the Other Side of the Disapprovals

In Jack Canfield's bestselling book, *The Success Principles*, he says that what the inner critic says comes from what our parents said to us growing up, except we never heard the reasoning behind their often harsh words.

For example, a parent saying, "What do you think you're doing? You can't climb that tree!" may have been interpreted by the child as "Who do you think you are to think you can handle climbing that big tree?" What wasn't heard was the other side of that statement, which is "I love you and I don't want to see you get hurt."

Similarly, Dr. Susan Jeffers, whose work on fear education has transformed millions of lives, said in her book, *Feel the Fear and Do It Anyway*, that when she was young, her mom never let her ride a bike. As a child, Dr. Jeffers had always understood that rule as meaning she was not capable of riding a bike. Now, as an adult, it's easier to look back and realize that our parents were warning us of potential peril because they loved us. But, as a child, it's very easy to hear the words to mean that we can't trust ourselves.

The point: past conditioning plays a huge part in what your inner critic has to say to you.

## Seeking Validation and Acknowledgement

In addition to seeking approval, as social creatures, we also seek validation from our peers. Ever heard of peer-group pressure? Seeking acceptance is a form of seeking validation. As human beings we want to fit in, to belong.

We also crave acknowledgement. It feels good when someone says, "You did a great job!" Especially if it's coming from someone whom you respect.

In an interview at Stanford University, Oprah Winfrey said that in her line of work she has interviewed celebrities and known personalities all around the world, from Nelson Mandela to Beyonce Knowles, and the one response they ALL had in common at the end of their interviews was "Was that OK?" which led her to conclude that everyone seeks validation. It's normal.

We carry this conditioning into adulthood, seeking approval or validation from our bosses, our peers, our spouses, our friends, even our children.

So your internal critic puts a lot of pressure on you to get approval and validation from others, and berates you when you feel you performed less-than. That's the function of the inner critic.

**Past Unpleasant Experiences**

Have you ever had past experiences where you felt humiliated or disempowered in front of a group of people?

For example, when I was in high school, I was sitting in my economics class, talking to my friend Louise next to me when the teacher called on me, "Mary, what is the definition of interest rates?" I was stunned. All I could see were eyes, staring at me, waiting for an answer. My mind went blank, and all I could feel was my face getting hotter and hotter. And I knew as this was happening, my face was getting redder and redder.

After what seemed like forever, to make matters worse, Louise jumped in with the correct answer, gloating, all proud of herself. Especially as a teenager, when peer-group acceptance felt so important, I was deeply embarrassed and humiliated. Many of my public speaking workshop participants shared similar experiences from their past.

As a young person, those negative experiences that you had in front of a group of people do affect you. You remember them. This is a common experience. It is important to understand why these unpleasant experiences are so easily remembered.

## Why You Still Remember Those Bad Experiences Like They Were Yesterday

Have you ever had a similar experience? I'm willing to bet that not only did you have one, but you could recall the exact situation, moment by moment.

That's not a coincidence. That is how the brain works. Molecular biologist, Dr. John Medina, in his *New York Times* bestselling book *Brain Rules* explains that when an emotionally-charged incident happens, a chemical called dopamine is dumped into our system, which aids memory. In essence Medina explains that it's like "a Post-it Note that says, 'Remember this,' " or more importantly—remember this and never have that situation happen again. *Don't do THAT again!*

## Fear of Public Humiliation as Its Fuel

The inner critic uses past public humiliation moments as "fuel" to scare us into never repeating a painful experience again.

## Survival

Let me put it to you another way:

## Our Human Need of Belonging and Love

As human beings, we all have common needs that drive us. You may have heard of Maslow's hierarchy of human needs:

Maslow's Hierarchy of Human Needs

The lowest level of the pyramid shows the needs that must be met first, our basic needs. We have to have food, water, warmth, and rest. Without those we would not live.

When you're in front of a room, and it feels like a "you against all of them" situation, your fear of social rejection is suddenly heightened because the third level of need, "belongingness and love," is perceived to be threatened. Let's face it, in that moment, it can feel like you're up there all alone.

Especially if the situation is outside your comfort zone, then the audience can feel hostile. In those moments because our need of belonging is not met, our brain reacts accordingly: adrenaline rush, shortness of breath, racing heart.

This is what you're dealing with. You aren't imagining it. It's all happening. The situation is triggering very ancient and ingrained physiological responses. Your brain is responding to a perceived threat. It's not just you! As a human being, you're hardwired that way.

## Tribes and the Need for Belonging That Drives the Need for Social Acceptance

In caveman days, do you think you would have had a greater chance of survival if you lived in a tribe or by yourself? Of course, in a tribe. If you got sick or injured, the members of your tribe would hunt and bring food home for you. Therefore, from our earliest origins so many millennia ago, we've been programed to be social animals. It's in our very nature. Unconsciously we know that social acceptance and belonging is a good thing for us. By contrast, social rejection and being an outcast, all by yourself, is not.

## The Amygdala and Fight-Flight-Freeze

As humans we have a "lower" brain, sometimes called the "lizard" brain. It's there for survival reasons. As a part of this survival mechanism, we have a part of our brain called the amygdala. It's responsible for our fight-flight-freeze response.

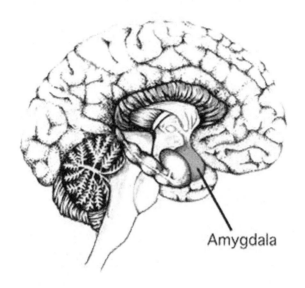

Amygdala

If our survival is perceived to be threatened, the amygdala's fight-flight-freeze response takes over our thinking brain temporarily and for good reason.

For example, if a stranger suddenly attacks you, you *want* the fight-flight-freeze response to take over. It reacts faster than you can think because its job is to get you the heck out of danger, so you can survive. The key word here is "survive."

The problem is when it's an audience in front of you and your physical survival is not threatened, but the perceived threat to one of your human needs, "belonging" is activated. Then this perceived threat can hijack your thinking brain and the amygdala takes over with its fight-flight-freeze response.

## How Does This Relate to Public Speaking?

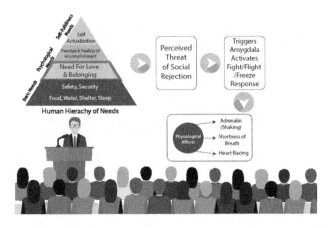

So relating this back to public speaking, let me ask you a question: when you are speaking in front of an audience, does it feel like you're part of the crowd? Or does it feel like you're all by yourself? When I ask this very question in my workshops, the unanimous response is always "By myself."

Think about it. There's the audience, facing you, and you're the only person facing all of them. All of their eyes are locked on you. And you are by yourself, looking at many eyes. Of course, it feels like you're alone. It feels like it's one of you against many of them.

That little voice in your head whispers to you, "I need them to like me. Don't reject me or else I'll be an outcast and I will die." Of course, you're not consciously thinking that. Your thinking, analytical brain, the prefrontal cortex, has temporarily been hijacked by your amygdala and the fight-flight-freeze mechanism.

Perhaps to your rational brain, what I'm explaining might sound very extreme, like an exaggeration, this fight-flight-freeze mechanism taking over when you speak in front of an audience. After all, even if you make a complete fool out of yourself, chances are you're not going to physically die on the spot. The thing to remember: all this brain activity from the amygdala is happening in your unconscious. You're not consciously thinking, "Must be accepted by tribe—or I will die," while you're in front of the room. It's your lizard brain sending out the simple message.

For example, I hear time and time again from my students: "When I get nervous in front of an audience, I go blank" or "I completely lose my train of thought." This is the amygdala doing its work, trying to save you from a perceived threat and doing so by "freezing" you.

So the trick here is to train yourself to recognize this fight-flight-freeze response when you're in front of an audience. Easier said than done, right? That's what we will talk about in detail in chapter 3, Empowering Yourself.

## Examining and Dissecting Fear

## The Misconception about Fear in Public Speaking

There is a misconception that people who are great public speakers were born that way, that they came out of the womb unafraid. Fortunately for me that misconception was broken early on in my own public speaking journey when I heard one of my favorite speaking mentors, Darren LaCroix, speak about his own journey. Darren showed a video of himself on stage giving his first ever stand-up comedy performance from many years ago. He was, by his own admission, extremely nervous and "terrible." From the video clip, it was obvious how nervous and self-conscious he was. He then showed his speech many years later that won him the 2001 World Champion of Public Speaking title.

My "aha"moment—even people who are masters at what they do were more than likely once afraid.

## Fear and Courage

One of my favorite speakers and authors is Dr.

Brené Brown. In a talk I saw her give at the Massachusetts Women's Conference, she said, and I'll paraphrase: there's a myth that if someone is courageous, then they feel no fear. That is incorrect. In fact, the opposite is true. Courage can only exist when there IS fear present. Otherwise there would be no need for courage.

In other words—courage is something you conjure up by acting in the face of fear.

Adam Markel, CEO of New Peaks, North America's largest personal and business development company that has trained over 1.5 million people from 104 countries, and author of *Pivot: The Art and Science of Reinventing Your Career and Life,* puts it this way, "Bravery isn't the feeling you get that allows you to take action. Bravery is what comes after. It's the tiny seed of confidence that grows a little more each time you take action . . . stop waiting to feel brave. There's no such thing."

## Tame the Cobra of Fear

Adam also teaches us to "tame the cobra of fear." Note that he doesn't say to "get rid of" or "kill" the cobra. He says TAME the cobra. It's natural to have fears and insecurities when speaking outside your comfort zone. Accept that fear will be there. Taking action despite fear is what it means to "tame the cobra of fear."

## Redefining the Meaning of Fear

In Dr. Susan Jeffers book *Feel the Fear and Do It Anyway*, she writes,

> While fear may look and feel like a psychological problem, in most cases it isn't. I believe it is primarily an educational problem and that by reeducating the mind, you can accept fear as simply a fact of life rather than a barrier to success. (This should be a relief to all of you out there who have been wondering "What's wrong with me?")

Dr. Jeffers' advice can be summed up in one phrase, which happens to be the title of her book: "Feel the fear and do it anyway."

## Fear or Excitement

Personal development teacher and author of *Heart Virtues*, Greg Moors Montana says that fear is actually excitement. He coached me that in the times when I'm scared, to say out loud to myself, "It's not fear—it's excitement."

Dave, a friend who is a seasoned sky diver, agrees with this idea. Dave once said to me, "Mary, did you know that the chemicals in your body when you feel fear are actually the same as when you feel excited"? This piqued my curiosity, so I looked it up and found that Dave was spot-on. In an article on WebMD, *Extreme Sports: What's the Appeal?*, Justin Anderson, PsyD, a sports consultant for the Center for Sports Psychology in Denton, Texas, says of people who play extreme sports: "They get a lot of adrenaline by it, and gravitate towards activities that give them that feeling. For some it's jumping out of airplanes, for others it's climbing Mt. Everest, and for others, it's the Ironman."

And guess what happens in your body when you are in fear? An article in the *Huffington Post* reveals, "Adrenaline . . . Commonly known as the fight or flight hormone, it is produced by the adrenal glands after receiving a message from the brain that a stressful situation has presented itself."

Wow! That's a revelation. You mean it's up to me to interpret whether the jittery sensations I'm feeling mean fear or excitement? I will choose excitement over fear any day.

## Ego

In connecting with an audience, in order to have impact there is no room for ego. Here's the deal with the ego. It has a very narrow agenda for you: "I want to look good" and "I don't want to look bad." And that's it.

Both items on this agenda come from fear, the fear of not wanting to look bad. When the ego is pushing its fear-based agenda, it steers you to focus on yourself rather than be there to serve the audience. If your highest intent in speaking is to serve the audience, then the fear of looking bad will evaporate because you are starting from a place of service (wanting to add value to your audience and help your audience) versus serving your ego (me, me, me).

If the ego is in the *driver's seat* when you are speaking to an audience, the audience will sense that you are there for your own glory, rather than to add value to them.

As human beings, we all have egos. The point is not to eliminate the ego. There's no such surgery as an ego-ectamy. The point again is to notice it when it comes up, so it's not driving you unconsciously.

**Fear of Judgment**

Most people are not afraid of public speaking because they fear it puts their life in peril, meaning they will risk death through it. They are afraid of public judgment. You saw in the earlier sections of this chapter why this is the case:

- Past conditioning from authority figures, like our parents, leads us to seek approval and validation.
- We have an amygdala that's responsible for our fight-flight-freeze response if we "perceive" danger. And public speaking can "feel" dangerous because we are hardwired to need social acceptance in order to survive. Public speaking puts us in the opposite place where we are making ourselves very vulnerable to social rejection—something our brains have been programmed to fear.
- Hence, people are not afraid of public speaking. They are afraid of public judgment.

## Women and the Need to Be Liked

At a conference in Oregon, when I met Kathleen Gage, a marketing guru, I asked, "Kathleen, you work with a lot of women. What's the one thing they have in common that holds them back?"

She thought about it and replied, "Fear of not being liked."

A few months later, I attended a communications course for women. The trainer, Myriam Jacobs, enlightened us to the fact that men are biologically driven by testosterone. They are hardwired to use their physical strength. The "dark side" of this nature is violence.

Conversely, women are biologically driven by oxytocin. It plays a role in social bonding. The "dark side" of that is being possessive in the bond, i.e., "She's MY friend, not YOUR friend!" This concept is what movies, like *Mean Girls*, and books, like *Queen Bees and Wannabes*, are based on. The cruelty of cliques that teenage girls are so popularly known for in high school stems from biology too.

Also, this is where women's need to be liked comes from—biology.

Why am I telling you all of this?

Because I want you to be aware of it. I believe the need to be liked extends beyond just women and to men as well because it's related to the need for acceptance, which is a basic human need, regardless of gender.

## Applying This Awareness to Public Speaking

When you're public speaking, it's important to be aware of your human predisposition to want to be liked. This awareness may play out like this: *It would be nice to be liked, and it's my preference to be liked, but that's not why I'm speaking. I am not driven by the need for your acceptance. I'm speaking to serve the audience and to add value.*

You will never be an effective public speaker if you are driven by the need to be liked. Here's the harsh reality: not everyone will like your message and not everyone will like you. You have to be OK with that. And this is especially true in the case of women. This is not a sexist comment. This is based on biological wiring. The antidote is not to deny it, but to be aware of it and speak anyway.

## Thoughts

According to a *Huffington Post* article, "There Are 50,000 Thoughts Standing Between You and Your Partner Every Day", an average person has about 50,000 thoughts per day. That's A LOT of thoughts.

If I put the thoughts in your head out loud on a speaker, it would be very noisy . . . random thoughts, one thought leading to another leading to another. It's much too easy to allow your attention to follow these arising thoughts and get sucked into a rat hole.

In my workshops, I pick up a bottle of water and ask my participants to shout out what comes to mind when they see the bottle of Fiji brand water. I hear words, like "thirst," "expensive," "clear," "half empty," "half full," etc. I then demonstrate what can go through my mind when I see this bottle of water:

*Fiji—beautiful island, blue waters, my sister and I once spoke about going to Fiji for a vacation. When I was living in Sydney, Fiji was so much closer. I live in Boston now. Come to think of it, I haven't spoken to my sister in quite a while. I hope she's doing OK. We should speak more often. I should make it a point to call her.*

At this point, my students are usually giggling because they can see how a simple bottle of water can cause a cascade of thoughts, and without being intentionally focused, I could easily end up chasing thoughts on auto-pilot.

Here's an example of how your thoughts might sound during public speaking:

*I'm so nervous, I hope I don't look nervous. Oh no, Rachel is in the audience, she is an expert on this topic. She will think this is too simple. What if someone asks a question that I don't know? Then I will look like a fool, and I don't want to look stupid.*

Can you relate to that? Of course, you can. Do you know how I know? Because you're not the only person who's ever had these kinds of thoughts. It's a common phenomenon.

## Self-Consciousness

As I shared in chapter 1, I was very self-conscious speaking in front of an audience and even one-on-one with people. I couldn't get my focus off of myself. My thoughts were consumed with fear of how the audience or the other person would notice all the flaws in me. It was torturous. It took a lot of energy to be consumed in worry like that.

And my self-consciousness wasn't just during presentations or in one-on-ones at work. I was very socially awkward. In my first job out of college, I was hired as a programmer by a prestigious bank. Every month, the department would throw a mandatory "coffee and snacks" afternoon during which the employees would mingle with one another and the management team. In these get-togethers, people would stand around in a big room, talking. I hated those events. I felt awkward.

This was before I learned about my little voice. I had been listening to the inner critic, who was whispering things to me, like "You're a fraud," "You'll make a fool out of yourself," or "Who do you think you are? There are other people more qualified than you," and I thought that these voices were telling "the truth."

Maybe you've had similar experiences? If so, it should be comforting to know that I got over that extreme discomfort by changing myself from the inside out, doing everything that I'm sharing with you in this book. And so can you.

## Shame

Researcher Dr. Brené Brown is an expert on shame and vulnerability. I recommend watching her TED talks:

- Listening to shame.
  http://www.ted.com/talks/brene_brown_lis tening_to_shame
- Vulnerability.
  http://www.ted.com/talks/brene_brown_on _vulnerability

Dr. Brown explains that shame prevents us from true connection.

To me, shame is a feeling that there's some part of myself that I want to reject, mixed with feeling like I did something wrong, mixed with the feeling that there's something wrong with me. Maybe you can relate to some of these feelings?

To extrapolate on this idea in terms of public speaking: if you have hidden shame, it could be preventing you from truly connecting with the audience. It's a barrier that prevents you from accepting yourself fully.

Also, Dr. Brown says that shame likes to be kept in the dark.

## It's Not Just You

*It's Not just You* is the title of Dr. Brené Brown's book on her findings about shame. As the title suggests, her research found that shame is experienced universally by all of us. And it's especially insidious and destructive because no one wants to talk about it because of the nature of how shame makes us feel. In her book she says shame is a "silent epidemic" and "People have been taught and socialized not to discuss [their shame] but we just keep pretending that it's not happening."

## Shame and Public Speaking

You might be thinking, "But, Mary, what has my shame about stuff from my past got to do with my public speaking?" Here's what I've learned: you cannot compartmentalize yourself. YOU are the common denominator. When you are in front of an audience, true connection means having nothing between you and your audience. Shame stories that you have about yourself can prevent you from owning your true power, both on and off stage, and, therefore, can create an invisible barrier between you and your audience.

A friend shared with me once that he was so petrified to speak in public because he was anticipating shame. The mere thought of having the shameful feeling sent him trembling. This friend went to great lengths to avoid scenarios where he might have to speak in public.

When I asked why this was the case, he shared with me an incident that happened to him at work. In a team meeting, he was called on to answer a simple question that he says, "Everyone should know." But he did not know the answer. He shared with me how ashamed he was to have been "found out" in front of all of his esteemed colleagues and boss.

Do you see how closely related shame can be to someone's avoidance of public speaking? Do you see how *being afraid of being ashamed* can put you in a miserable and lonely prison?

## Shame as Fuel for the Little Voice of the Inner Critic

In *It's Not Just You*, Dr. Brené Brown writes,

We can't silence the old tape in our head that suddenly blares some version of "something is wrong with me." For example, that imposter or phony feeling at work or school rarely has anything to do with our abilities, but has more to do with that fearful voice inside of us that scolds and asks, "Who do you think you are?" Shame forces us to put so much value on what other people think that we lose ourselves in the process of trying to meet everyone else's expectations.

## Shame, the Little Voice, and the Lowest Level Beliefs

I know what you're thinking, "Come on, Mary, you're telling me about our little voice and the inner critic, and now we have this shame thing to think about too? Mary, there better be some good news here . . ."

Guess what? There is.

## Antidote to Shame

Dr. Brené Brown's research found that the antidote to shame is empathy. Shame likes to be kept in the dark, and empathy sheds light on it.

But you don't go talking to any old stranger about your shame. You talk with someone who has earned your trust over time, like a close friend. Professional psychotherapists can also help you unravel your shame stories.

## How to Work through Shame on Your Own When It Comes Up

I find that if I'm feeling shame, there's usually a limiting self-belief lurking just underneath. This is when journaling helps me. I use free writing to "brainstorm" what the little voices of my inner critic are saying about that shameful feeling. For example, they might be telling me, "You could have done better," "Why didn't you speak up?" or "You're a loser."

Once I have these little voices pinned down, I can now objectively narrow down and determine the root little voice that's causing these shameful feelings.

So if I find that "You're a loser" best matches the feeling of that shame, then I can look more deeply into it and ask myself, "What is the underlying limiting self-belief that spurs this little voice, 'You're a loser'?" And more often than not, it's the limiting self-belief "I'm not good enough."

Then I put this limiting self-belief, "I'm not good enough," through the 3Rs Process, dismantle it, and reframe into an empowering belief, "I am good enough." (In chapter 3, I carefully explain the 3Rs Process and we look at many examples of limiting self-beliefs too.)

In a sense, through this journaling, I am giving empathy to myself by looking deeply within and seeing for myself what the core disempowering belief is that's making me feel shame.

The next time you feel a shameful feeling, whether related to public speaking or not, I recommend brainstorming to see what your little voices are saying and then see if you can uncover a limiting self-belief. You can use *Worksheet #3: Brainstorming Your Little Voices around Shame* in the companion workbook. Once you identify that limiting self-belief lurking under the shame, run it through the 3R Process that you'll find in chapter 3.

## External Critics

Yes, external critics exist too. I'd love to sugarcoat it for you and tell you they don't. But they do.

The external critic comes in all shapes and sizes. They are the people who give you negative feedback. Some are well-intended, some are not. Sometimes you have asked for the feedback, and sometimes the feedback is unsolicited.

For example, in 2009, during my year-long journey to the World Championship of Public Speaking, I rehearsed in front of many audiences. During one rehearsal, I was feeling particularly low. I didn't connect well with the audience. I was agitated because the finals were only one week away. Something was missing, and in that moment I didn't know what it was.

When the rehearsal session ended, a middle-aged man came up to me and asked, "When are the finals? Next week?" I nodded. He put one hand on my shoulder and said—and I quote—"There's always next year." He was implying that, based on the rehearsal, he had already written me off as a realistic contender. He may as well have said, "You don't have a chance." I won't lie, that comment stung me. Especially because I was already in a low emotional space.

Three days later, I was at my second-to-last rehearsal before the actual contest. After I asked for feedback, a man in his 30s, wearing a shirt and khaki pants, stood up from his seat, projected his voice loudly, and announced with great gusto—and I quote—"You have no content!"

Not only was that comment delivered with no tact, but it was also not constructive.

Why am I telling you this?

Because external critics are out there. Especially when you ASK them for their feedback.

If their comments sting you, it's OK. It's a good sign because you know you are still human. No one wants to hear a robot speak. They want to hear from someone who is human, just like they are—with vulnerabilities and insecurities just like they have. If you don't feel any emotion, it's unlikely the audience can relate to you.

We'll talk more about feedback in chapter 6, The Process of Mastery. For now, feedback can be a great mechanism for improvement. My suggestion is to treat feedback as a gift. You can use it, or you can throw it away. Once it's given to you, you can decide what to do with it.

If someone gives you a really ugly shirt for your birthday, you say, "Thank you." Then when they leave, you can shove it into a drawer and never look at it again, donate it, or throw it in the trash. It's yours to decide what you want to do with it. You don't force yourself to wear it and feel awful about how ugly you look!

That's how feedback works. It's not the truth. You get to decide if you want to take it on. My suggestions are:

1.  Re-look at the feedback objectively when you are calm.
    —And—

2.  Ask yourself, "Is there merit to what they are telling me?"

## CHAPTER 2 GOLDEN NUGGETS

To become a better public speaker, invest in getting to know yourself better, the conscious and subconscious realms:

- With the intention of better understanding ourselves, we shine a light into those dark areas within that we unknowingly avoid.

- We fear judgment and seek approval and validation—not because there's something wrong with us but because that's the nature of being human.

- Being nervous is a natural response to being outside of our comfort zone.

- We, as humans, want to look good and avoid looking bad. It's called the ego.

- We each have an inner critic whose job it is to say things that keep us from leaving our comfort zone. Its "little voices" discourage us from growing because the inner critic sees growing as scary and uncertain. It thinks it is protecting us. The inner critic and its discouraging voices are not inherently a bad thing; it's just how we're wired—to survive.

- Understanding fear and how that's a perfectly human emotion is useful because we can act in spite of the fear.

- The antidote to the little voices is *awareness and action*. Parry their punches to the side and act anyway.

# CHAPTER 3

# EMPOWERING YOURSELF

In the previous chapter we learned that nervousness and fear about public speaking stems from our survival instinct. We learned about the little voice, which comes from the inner critic. We also learned how to practice becoming aware of our internal critic, so we can take action to speak, in spite of it. Now, we can continue our growth from this new baseline.

In this chapter you will look further into shifting your mindset to empower yourself, and you'll learn how staying in that context of empowerment serves you as you grow as a public speaker. This is so important because when you slip into a disempowering context, which can commonly happen along the public speaking journey, you need to know how to get yourself out of it and continue the journey.

An important part of this process involves those little voices from the inner critic. We will dive deeper into the underlying source of those little voices, your limiting self-beliefs. To do so, I will take you through a simple process I call the "3Rs." You can use the 3Rs over an over again to debunk the negative messages of those little voices in order to reframe any limiting self-beliefs.

I will share some very practical tactics that I've implemented in my life to encourage self-awareness and self-empowerment. These handy tools will help you to keep flowing in the empowering context of trusting yourself, and they will give you a gentle kick in the butt to snap you out of the trance of feeling bad about yourself that happens when you slip into a disempowering funk.

Once you have these tools in your tool belt, you can begin to adopt the techniques that make the most sense to you and implement them to become a better public speaker.

Finally, in this chapter, we look at concrete ways to build self-trust.

## Working on You

When the late "father of motivation" Jim Rohn was asked, "How do you develop an above-average income?" he responded, "Simple. Become an above-average person—Work on you." And that is also what I would say about developing an above-average public speaking ability—*work on yourself*.

In this chapter, Empowering Yourself, and in chapter 6, The Process of Mastery, we address quite deeply what working on yourself entails. Remember, it's not just about getting good at the "skill" of public speaking—that's only half the jigsaw puzzle. The other half is working on you, the vessel of the delivery, so you're no longer in your own way. Instead, you can be fully present and ready to connect with your audience.

Working on you means knowing what you need to work on, which can partly be revealed through self-reflection.

## Be Self-Reflective

I love to study the masters of various crafts as a means of uncovering the master's mindset. For example, do you remember the tennis great Billy Jean King? If you haven't heard of her, Billy Jean King, in the 1960s and 70s, won 39 Grand Slam titles. If you're not familiar with the tennis world, I really want you to get the magnitude of that achievement.

There are four Grand Slams in a year: the US Open, the Australian Open, the French Open, and Wimbledon. World-class tennis players from around the world work their butts off to try and win just one Grand Slam, and most of them never do. And here is this woman, Billy Jean King, who won 39 Grand Slams in her career. Here's what Billy Jean King had to say:

---

## SELF-AWARENESS IS PROBABLY THE MOST IMPORTANT THING TOWARDS BEING A CHAMPION.

---

To me, a champion is someone who strives to reach their own potential, and you don't have to be winning any trophies to do that. In public speaking, it would be becoming the best speaker you can be.

$$|\ -\ -\ -\ -\ \blacktriangleright\ \text{Gap}\ \blacktriangleleft\ -\ -\ -\ -\ |$$

Your **Current**                     Your
Skill Level                     **Potential**

In the diagram above, the left line represents where we are currently in our skill level as a public speaker (or any skill), and the right line represents our potential. There's this gap in between. We need to work to bridge that gap—and self-awareness is crucial in doing so.

How do we know what we need to work on if we're not self-aware?

The answer: self-reflection.

We will investigate self-reflection in more detail in chapter 6, The Process of Mastery. For now, understand that looking at yourself is necessary to improve as a public speaker because you are the common denominator in all your experiences.

## There's Nothing Wrong with You

As you learned in chapter 2, the amygdala in the human brain has the job of scanning for threats, so, by default, the brain is wired for survival. Even still, don't believe everything your mind tells you.

As human beings, we sometimes have self-doubts, insecurities, and, as we discussed, negative little voices in our heads. These insecurities tend to surface more prominently when we step outside of our comfort zone, such as speaking in front of a group of people, particularly if the presentation is very important to us. That's when the little voices of self-doubt rear their ugly heads.

What you must remember is that this is totally normal. There is nothing wrong with you. Being very nervous is just a sign that adrenalin is pumping into your system. What you must not allow yourself to do is jump to conclusions and buy into those insecurities. Don't believe those little voices of your inner critic. It's just an ancient part of the human brain expressing itself and thinking it is helping—but, in fact, in this situation at least, it is behind the times and hindering you.

## Comfortable in Your Own Skin

Being comfortable in your own skin means being the driver of your experiences despite the nagging backseat driver that is the inner critic. And whatever you do, don't compare yourself to anyone else. Comparison is usually being done by the ego part of you.

Instead, practice this mindset: everyone is exactly where they are supposed to be. We are all equals. What you have to say is just as valid as the next person. Do not devalue yourself or wish you were something else that you're not. This point is best illustrated by the short fable below:

One day in the green fields, a squirrel saw a giraffe, nibbling leaves off of a tall tree. The squirrel thought, "I wish I were a giraffe, so tall and graceful, able to reach leaves without ever climbing anything."

Meanwhile, the giraffe was thinking, "I wish I were a squirrel, small and nimble, being able to climb high up on a tree to hide from predators. I, on the other hand, stick out like a sore thumb."

Can you see how ridiculous this line of thinking is? A giraffe is beautiful and unique, and so is a squirrel, in its own right. Since neither one can "become" the other, spending time "wishing" it were so is just a waste of energy.

## Get Over Yourself

I attended a public speaking workshop with one of my favorite mentors, Ed Tate, the 2000 World Champion of Public Speaking. In the workshop, he had all of his participants repeat after him the following three phrases. I'd like you to say them out loud now:

- *I look like that.*
- *I sound like that.*
- *Get over it.*

Of course, we all laughed, because as soon as we said them out loud, we recognized the truth of each statement and the ridiculousness of it all at the same time.

No one likes the way they look or sound most of the time, and it's OK because you're there to impart a message to the audience, not to "look good."

## Focus on Your Strengths

In chapter 2, we explored how all human beings have fears and doubts. It's simply part of the human experience. As a result, we hesitate to put ourselves outside of our comfort zones.

We saw that, as humans, the need to be accepted and, therefore, fear of rejection are part of our genetic code. Fear of judgment is there, ingrained in our very DNA; thus, the insecurities we have about ourselves seem magnified.

You need to look at yourself objectively. The keyword here is "objectively," as in—without listening to the little voice of your inner critic. Here's the fun part—looking at yourself also means seeing what you're *good* at, acknowledging what comes naturally and easily to you and the skills you have that you've worked hard on and now possess. These are elements you ought to be aware of and leverage in your public speaking and in your everyday life.

## Using Your Strengths in Public Speaking

Let's take a look at your strengths and how you can leverage them in public speaking. What are your strengths in public speaking? Get clear on what your top strengths are.

For example, when I was competing in the World Championship of Public Speaking, I reached out to the 2007 past World Champion, Vikas Jhingran. I asked, "Vikas, I made it to the World Championship finals. What advice do you have for me?"

He answered me with a question: "Mary, what are your strengths? Write your speech around your strengths." I had no idea what my strengths were. I had to go away and think about it.

---

## WRITE YOUR SPEECH AROUND YOUR STRENGTHS.

### —VIKAS JHINGRAN, 2007 WORLD CHAMPION OF PUBLIC SPEAKING

---

I asked myself, "What are my strengths? What comes naturally to me? What do I do that the audience responds to consistently?" Upon reflection, I isolated three things:

1. I'm naturally a silly person. (It took me many years to be able to show my silliness on stage. I used to be very serious. But that's another story . . .)
2. I've heard multiple people tell me that I'm *animated* and have a very expressive face, a *plastic* face, if you will.
3. And my nephew told me he likes how I do "voices."

I took Vikas's advice—and not just for my World Championship speech. You'll never see me give a speech without being silly, using my animated face, and embellishing in voices, because these are my strengths.

Here are some more examples of what people have identified as their strengths from my workshop participants. Their strengths include:

- *I'm always prepared.*
- *I'm humorous.*
- *I project my voice well.*
- *I can fake confidence when I need to.*
- *I know my topic.*
- *I'm conversational.*
- *I'm interactive with my audience.*
- *I use visuals and props.*
- *I'm passionate.*

- *I have good vocal variety.*
- *I've been told I sound sincere.*
- *I've been told I have a nice smile.*
- *I make sure I dress well.*

My question to you, "What are your top three strengths in public speaking?" Either strengths you already know about or that other people have pointed out to you. Write these down. You can use *Worksheet #4: Focusing on Your Strengths* in your companion workbook. And remember that the goal is for you to incorporate these strengths into your presentations.

## Strengths as Declarations

As mentioned in chapter 2, in my workshops, participants explore their strengths more fully when they do the Deck of 52 Strengths Exercise. When I have people in my classes share their strengths with the group, the words I commonly hear are humble descriptors on the modest side, such as "friendly," "optimistic," "hardworking." They rarely deliver bold claims, like "magnificent," "terrific," or "amazing."

So, I have the class shout out 10 bold words. For example, the list of bold words that the group comes up with might look like this:

- Magnificent
- Terrific
- Amazing
- Awesome
- Fantastic
- Wonderful
- Miraculous
- Fabulous
- Captivating
- Brilliant

I'll ask you what I ask my workshop participants now: choose from the list above the word that best resonates with you about yourself, and then to write it down as a declarative statement in the following way:

My name is _____.

And I am _____!

For example, my declaration would be:

*My name is Mary.*

*And I am magnificent!*

## The Power of a Declaration—No Evidence Necessary

Say your declaration out loud. When doing so, notice what your little voice is saying in response. It might say, "I feel silly" or "This feels ridiculous" or "No, I'm not." And here is why a declaration is so powerful.

A declaration is like sticking a flag into the ground and *declaring* to the universe, "This is the way it is"—no evidence, justification, or explanation is needed. It doesn't hinge on any past accomplishments that "deem" or "qualify" you to be what you are declaring. You are creating that into the world and then "living into it." You are making it so simply through the act of declaring.

In my workshops, I ask each person to stand up, one by one, and make their declaration out loud to the class, like they mean it. The more you can get your emotions involved in the declaration, the stronger you will feel it.

Inevitably, I hear giggles in the room because their little voices might be saying, "This is going to feel weird" or "I feel embarrassed, like I'm boasting." Of course, these feelings might come up because how often do we make bold claims like that? Hardly ever if at all! And that's exactly what

I want you to get comfortable with, making that bold claim and meaning it: YES, I AM AMAZING/FANTASTIC/MAGNIFICENT.

In my workshops after a person states their declaration the class gives a loud applause, as a sign of support that the person is what they declared.

Own it!

How?

By standing up and declaring it out loud to the universe.

Stand up now and say out loud your declaration. I'll even do it with you.

Ready? One, two, three—go: *My name is Mary. And I am magnificent!*

Great job!

## Declarations to Become a Better Speaker

Put your hand on your heart and repeat after me, out loud:

*My Name is [your name].*

*And I am [brilliant/magnificent/amazing]!*

*I will do whatever it takes to become the speaker I know I can become, starting with reading this book and completing the exercises.*

*I will look back in five years time and not recognize myself.*

## Limiting Self-Beliefs

A limiting self-belief is a disempowering statement that you think is the "truth" that sits strongly but under a cloak in your self-concept. It's a mental *blind spot* that you can't seem to get around. It's something you told yourself a long time ago and have been a hostage to ever since.

Each limiting self-belief is like a heavy piece of luggage you're carrying around with you, unnecessarily and often even unknowingly. It's time to reveal how they got there in the first place, and that's what this section is all about.

We all have limiting self-beliefs, and I want to help you to look at yours. I've certainly worked a lot on mine and continue to do so. Let's examine limiting self-beliefs in more detail to understand them better. Also, we'll look at some common ones and how they can impact you in public speaking.

## Look under the Layers to Find the Source of Limiting Self-Beliefs

People that come to me have the intention to improve their public speaking ability. Many want to feel more confident in presentations. So, I ask them questions, such as:

- *What's stopping you from having full confidence right now?*
- *What's there for you when you don't have confidence?*

After having trained thousands of people and coached hundreds of individuals in public speaking, I started to see a pattern in people's responses. When I dig down a little, what I find, buried under several layers of answers, is usually a limiting self-belief.

A limiting self-belief is commonly in this format:

- I'm not _____ enough.
- I'm too _____ .

### Common Limiting Self-Beliefs

Below are some limiting self-beliefs that have been identified and shared by my workshop participants about themselves. Can you relate to any of them?

- *I'm not good enough.*
- *I'm not smart enough.*
- *I'm not qualified enough.*
- *I'm not self-confident enough.*
- *I'm not clear enough.*
- *I'm not funny enough.*
- *I'm not courageous enough.*
- *I can't think on my feet.*
- *I'm not perfect enough.*
- *People will judge me if I make a mistake.*
- *I'm not pretty/handsome enough.*
- *I'm not brave enough.*
- *My English is not good enough.*
- *I'm too shy.*
- *I'm too quiet.*
- *I'm too inexperienced.*
- *I'm too old.*
- *I'm too young.*
- *I'm too busy to work on my presentations.*
- *I'm not animated enough.*
- *I'm not serious enough.*

And limiting self-beliefs can get even more specific. For example, a woman in one of my workshops shared that one of her limiting self-beliefs was "My brother is the smart one. I'm the dumb one." A man in a workshop once shared this when reflecting on his limiting self-beliefs: "I have a lot to live up to with my siblings' achievements. I'm the youngest of four siblings, and my elder siblings are each very successful—a doctor, a lawyer, and a pharmacist."

The theme of limiting self-beliefs can be similar, but where the belief itself came from is very specific to the person. I've trained people with master's degrees and PhDs, who identified their limiting self-belief as "I'm not smart enough," which shows that there is often no rationale behind limiting self-beliefs.

## The Little Voices That Stem from Your Limiting Self-Beliefs

Often, your limiting self-beliefs may not be immediately obvious to you. Instead, they will manifest as little voices on a related theme. For example, if your limiting self-belief is "I'm not good enough," the little voices that stem from that might include:

- *I'm not ready yet.*
- *I don't want to fail.*
- *Who do I think I am?*
- *I'm not qualified (especially when presenting to superiors).*
- *I will fail.*
- *Someone else can do it better than I can.*

## How Do Limiting Self-Beliefs Affect You during Public Speaking?

In any situation where you're communicating with a group of people, you have an audience. And it's not necessarily a "formal" presentation. You could be speaking up during a work meeting or networking with people at a conference. Perhaps, your audience includes your boss, co-workers, clients, or peers.

If you don't become aware of your own limiting self-beliefs and release yourself from them, while you're on the platform, those beliefs will create an invisible "wall" between you and the audience. So, instead of being *with* the audience in the here and now, what you're unconsciously focused on are those little voices in your head that stem from the limiting self-beliefs.

For example, the voices might be saying things, like "What are they going to think of me?" or "Can they tell I'm a fake?" These voices distract your attention away from your message and the audience, thus making your delivery of the message and connection with the audience much weaker.

## Your Limiting Self-Beliefs Affect Your Tapestry

Here's another important reason why it would benefit you to address your limiting self-beliefs: imagine a tapestry or a large piece of fabric. If there was a loose thread dangling from the edge of the fabric and you start to pull on it, what happens to the rest of the fabric? It starts to shrink, right?

Your limiting self-beliefs are like those loose threads on the fabric. We have many threads. Our job is to be on the lookout for those threads when they reveal themselves and run them through the 3Rs Process that I'm about to show you, so you can release them. You are figuratively cutting those loose threads off, so the exquisite tapestry is revealed in all its magnificence to your audience.

I can assure you that whatever your limiting self-beliefs are, they don't just affect you when you're public speaking. They also come up in other areas of your life, especially when you're out of your comfort zone, because you are the common denominator.

On the upside, the opposite is also true. When you address limiting self-beliefs as you see them and recognize them for what they really are—illusions of the mind—you will become much more confident as a public speaker, and that confidence seeps into other areas of your life as well.

## The 3Rs Process—To Get Past Your Limiting Self-Beliefs

So how do you go about identifying and busting your own limiting self-beliefs? It's a process I call the "3Rs." This three-step process supplies you with a tool to further examine and debunk your limiting self-beliefs.

### The 3Rs—Step 1—REFLECT

The first R in the 3Rs Process stands for *reflect*. So let's do that. Right now, reflect on the following question:

# WHAT ARE SOME LIMITING SELF-BELIEFS THAT YOU HAVE?

There is no right or wrong response here. There are probably a few that you can immediately identify that hold you back.

After *reflecting* write down at least one limiting self-belief that you have, whether it's related to public speaking or not. Again, there's no right or wrong. Write down the first one that comes to mind.

You can always come back and add to this step as you uncover more. You can even choose ones from the above section, "Common Limiting Self-Beliefs." For example, one limiting self-belief that comes up for me sometimes is "What I have to say is not important." Now, it's your turn!

*Your Turn*: write down a limiting self-beliefs that you have. In the workbook, you can use *Worksheet #5: The 3Rs Process* to record your response. Do that now.

### The 3Rs—Step 2—RECALL

The second R stands for *recall.*

*What was the earliest moment in your life when you first remember having the thought of this limiting self-belief?*

For me, the first time I had the thought, "What I have to say is not important," was in the third grade, back in Australia where I grew up. I was sitting in a class of 25 kids. A substitute teacher, Mr. McDonald, announced, "Class, today we're going to tell each other jokes. Who has a joke and wants to come up to the front of the class and tell it?"

Everyone raised their hands. Mr. McDonald called a student to go in front of the class. The student told a joke and then sat back down. One by one Mr. McDonald called on my classmates. They each went up and told a joke. He called every person in the class. I was the last hand up who hadn't been called.

Just when it was my turn, Mr. McDonald stated, "That's all we have time for." There I was, in the back of the classroom. In that moment, as an 8-year-old, I had the thought and decided, "I guess what I have to say is not very important."

In this *recalling* second step of the 3Rs Process, I saw that I was a little 8-year-old when this thought, this limiting self-belief, first got into my head. And I carried that thought with me like it was true, all the way into my adult life. And that is just one limiting self-belief. I have many others.

By *recalling* the first time you had that limiting self-belief, you get to see that you, yourself, are the source of the limiting self-belief. No one else. Before that point you did not have that limiting self-belief. You were not "born" with it. You made an interpretation and deemed it true.

In my example, for all I know, Mr. McDonald was rushing home to have a beer and ended class early. Or maybe he was oblivious. And I will never know. Whatever reason he had to not choose me, I was the one who made up that thought, "What I have to say is not important." Nobody else. I am the source of that limiting self-belief.

Here are a few more examples from my workshop participants:

*Rebecca,* a college professor, *reflected* and saw she had a limiting self-belief that she "wasn't good enough." When she *recalled,* she remembered that in kindergarten, her teacher asked everyone to draw a cat. Rebecca didn't know how to draw a cat. She looked to either side of her, and her classmates were all drawing cats with ease. She started to panic. In that moment, she created the thought that she "wasn't good enough."

*Rick*, a successful director in a company and an ex-military man, *reflected* and saw he had a limiting self-belief that he "wasn't smart enough." When he *recalled*, he remembered that in the first grade, his teacher asked everyone to write one paragraph about school. Rick's mind went blank. He forgot what a paragraph was and was too afraid to ask because his teacher was a grumpy woman to begin with. He just sat there, panicking internally. All he managed to write was the word "school." At the end of class his teacher came to collect his paper, and, as Rick had suspected, she yelled at him, "What's this? Just one word?" In that moment, Rick created the thought that he "wasn't smart enough."

*William*, a PhD student, *reflected* and saw he had a limiting self-belief that he "was ugly." When he *recalled*, he remembered that in junior high school, he asked a girl out to a dance and she said no. He then asked a another girl out who also said no. He lost his nerve to ask a third girl. Instead, he created the thought that he "wasn't handsome enough."

Your turn to *recall*: using the limiting self-belief that you came up with when you *reflected* in step 1 to answer this question:

*Your Turn*: what was the earliest moment in your life when you first remember having that thought, i.e., that limiting self-belief?

Write it down. You can use your companion workbook, *Worksheet #5: The 3Rs Process* to record your response. Do that now.

### The 3Rs—Step 3—REFRAME

The third R in the 3Rs Process stands for *reframe*. And it is in this *reframe* step that the beautiful thing about the discovery you made in the *recall* step above occurs.

From step 2, can you now see that the limiting self-belief came from an earlier part of your life? In fact, you were the one who made that thought up. YOU WERE NOT BORN WITH IT. You picked it up somewhere along the way.

And if you picked it up somewhere along the way, doesn't it make sense that you can drop it and pick up a more empowering belief? But how do you do that? That's where step 3, the third R comes in—*reframe*.

Firstly, turn your limiting self-belief around and state the opposite by asking yourself this question:

*How can you reframe this limiting self-belief to be an empowering belief instead?*

For example: my limiting self-belief was *What I have to say is not important*. When I state the opposite, the statement becomes: *What I have to say* is *important*. And this is where the beauty of *reframing* starts to happen.

*Your Turn*: what is the opposite statement to your limiting self-belief? Write it down.

You can use *Worksheet #5: The 3Rs Process* in your companion workbook to write down your response. Do that now.

## Three Pieces of Evidence

The second part of this third step of *reframe* is for you to come up with three pieces of evidence to disprove the limiting self-belief and, instead, to support this new, empowering *reframed* statement.

For example, my *reframed* empowering statement is *What I have to say* is *important*. My three pieces of evidence to support this powerful *reframing* are the following:

- *Evidence 1*—I have coaching clients that have told me, "Mary, your words and coaching advice have really helped me and inspired me."
- *Evidence 2*—I speak professionally. People pay me to hear my words. To them what I have to say is of value.

- *Evidence 3*—I have friends who call to ask my opinion and advice on matters that are important to them. To these friends, what I have to say is of value.

Here are a few more examples from my workshop participants:

*Donna*, a successful business woman, *reflected* to identify her limiting self-belief: "I need to be perfect." Her *reframed* empowering self-belief was "I am who I am, and that is enough." Her three pieces of evidence to support this new empowering belief were:

1. I have colleagues who have always respected me.
2. I have family and friends who love me.
3. In my business, I know what I'm doing.

*Amanda*, is a manager in a large organization. Her limiting self-belief was "I'm stupid." Her *reframed* empowering self-belief was "I am smart enough." Her three pieces of evidence to support "I am smart enough" were:

1. I have a master's degree.
2. I raised three healthy children who are now contributing adults.

3. I created an after-school program for the children in my local area.

*Ann* is a successful financial consultant from China. Her limiting self-belief was "My English language is not good enough." Her *reframed* empowering self-belief was "My English language is good enough for what I do." Her three pieces of evidence to support her *reframed* empowering self-belief were:

1. I have taken many business writing trainings (in English), and my writing is better than the average business writer.
2. I've been hired by many of the top financial firms as a consultant.
3. I'm not afraid to ask questions when I don't understand. I am always willing to learn.

*Your Turn*: take a few minutes now to contemplate for yourself. For the empowering self-belief that you wrote down above, find 3 pieces of evidence to support it and disprove the original limiting self-belief.

Again, you can use *Worksheet #5: The 3Rs Process* to record your three pieces of evidence.

## Beliefs and Evidence

Once the belief was created in our mind, over the years, we unconsciously found evidence to continually support it. In essence, it's like a self-fulfilling prophecy.

To see what I mean, let me create a visual metaphor. Imagine your limiting self-beliefs sitting on top of a table. The legs of the table are the pieces of evidence that held up the limiting self-belief. And now it's time for you to cut off those table legs to topple that table top of the limiting self-belief to the floor.

For example, the limiting self-belief that I was looking at was "What I have to say is not important." Say, I'm in a conference meeting at work and feeling brave enough to talk. Then one of my co-workers interrupts me and hijacks the conversation. The inner critic in my mind might assert, "See, what I have to say is not important. I knew that was true." In this way my mind continues to play into that limiting self-belief by finding "evidence" for it.

So now, in this third step of the 3Rs, I asked you to identify three pieces of evidence to support that *new empowering* view. With each of the above pieces of new evidence that supports the empowering statement, you are figuratively cutting off one of the table legs that supported the original limiting self-belief. When you cut down three legs of a table, it will no longer be able to stand. It topples over. The whole limiting self-belief is no longer valid.

In my workshops, I have people write their original limiting self-belief on a small piece of paper. At the end of the 3Rs, I have them physically scrunch up the piece of paper and throw it across the room. They have fun doing this, and there is often laughter as they do it. They do this because it represents the physical "release" of that limiting self-belief—the toppling of the table.

You can do the same with your limiting self-belief. Write it down on a small piece of paper, then scrunch it up, and throw it in the trash as a symbol for having worked on and released it.

First—you *reframe* the old limiting self-belief, and next you finally release it.

Do you see how you can repeat the the 3Rs for *any* limiting self-belief that you have?

## Self-Policing Your Thoughts

Make it a point to police your thoughts and emotions. In chapter 5, Presence, we will look at how to do this in detail. For now, be on the look out and notice when you are feeling disempowered or down. Take a pause and ask yourself honestly, what you are thinking. Be the observer of your thoughts.

For example, before or after giving a speech or presentation, you notice you feel out of sorts. Pause and ask yourself, "What are my thoughts right now?" Get quiet and listen. Be honest with yourself. Catch your disempowering thoughts on the fly as they are happening. What are the little voices saying? You might find that the little voices are berating you by saying things like:

- *You could have done much better.*
- *You sucked.*
- *I can't believe you forgot to give point number 3. How could you have forgotten that?*

Now take a lesson from chapter 2 and use the Best Friend Test. If your best friend confided, "I just gave a presentation and I sucked!" would your response be, "You're right, you did suck!"? And if the answer is no, then why on earth would you say those things to YOURSELF? This is the Best Friend Test. By monitoring your thoughts and applying the Best Friend Test, you can snap the heck out of feeling down and negative.

## Little Voice Journal

To practice monitoring disempowering thoughts on a consistent basis, I highly recommend keeping a "little voice journal" (LVJ). This is how it works: when you notice a disempowering little voice come up, write it down in your LVJ. The act of writing it down creates a mental distance, a separation between you and the little voice. Once it's written down, you can then look at it objectively, question it, interrogate it, and ultimately prove it to be BS, meaning lies.

For example, you were motivated and volunteered for a presentation. As you're putting together the presentation, your little voice is saying:

- *What was I thinking? This is so much work.*
- *I'm not qualified to talk about this.*
- *Who did I think I was to volunteer?*
- *Everyone's going to know I'm a fraud.*

Your LVJ (little voice journal) can be a physical journal or a digital version, e.g., the notepad on your smart phone or a computer document or all of the above. I use all three formats to make it very convenient and accessible on a moment-to-moment basis. Another option: you can use *Worksheet #6: Little Voice/Empowerment Journal* in your companion workbook.

The format of the journal entries doesn't matter. The important thing is to write down the disempowering words and see them in front of you. Once they are in front of you, run them through the Best Friend Test. Ask yourself, "Would my best friend say these things to me?" If the answer is no, then know that it's probably your lizard brain, trying to protect you from danger, stopping you from going outside of your comfort zone. It's the voice of your inner critic.

So often when we hear these little voices, we automatically believe them. The key then is first hearing them and then debunking them. You must practice in order to even hear them.

So, when you hear these voices, write them down in your little voice journal. The idea here is to catch the little voices as they come up in real time. By writing them down, you're acknowledging them, as in, "Yes, I hear you. Thank you for your concern. I know your intention is to keep me safe and within my comfort zone. I appreciate that. I am moving ahead anyway." In this way you're figuratively turning the light on in the dark room of your mind to reveal there are no real monsters under the bed. The monsters are only in your head. They are illusions.

Don't give in to the little voices. Instead—write them down. This is the first crucial step. And this works not just with the little voices pertaining to public speaking. When I was writing this book, I heard my little voices saying disempowering things to me, and I wrote them down in my LVJ. For example, they told me:

- *OMG my writing is so bad.*
- *I'm not inspired at all right now. This feels hard.*
- *I don't wanna write. No one is ever going to read this.*

The fact that you're reading this book is evidence that writing down those little voices works because, despite the voices, I completed and published this book that you're now reading.

I can't emphasize enough the importance of keeping an LVJ and writing in it as a habit. It's a muscle you're building that, when strong, you'll become faster and faster at catching the voices before they do damage, before they stop you from taking action.

### Empowerment Journal

This is the second crucial step for not allowing your inner critic to sabotage your continued motivation to become a better public speaker—the empowerment journal.

The empowerment journal is the opposite of your little voice journal. For every entry you write in your LVJ, you immediately write an entry in your empowerment journal that counters the message of the inner critic. If you have trouble coming up with anything empowering to write, ask yourself, "What would my best friend say to me?" Again, you can use *Worksheet #6: Little Voice/Empowerment Journal.*

Here are some example entries based on some common little voices people hear in public speaking and their empowering counterparts.

**Little Voice Journal Entry:** *What was I thinking? This is so much work.*

**Empowerment Journal Entry:** *Nothing ever worth achieving came easily.*

**Little Voice Journal Entry:** *I'm not qualified to speak on this topic. Who do I think I am?*

**Empowerment Journal Entry:** *I'll do the research necessary to come up to speed on this topic.*

**Little Voice Journal Entry:** *Everyone's going to know I'm a fraud.*

**Empowerment Journal Entry:** *There's no need to be paranoid. I know a lot more than I think and my intention is sincere.*

**Little Voice Journal Entry:** *I sucked in that presentation.*

**Empowerment Journal Entry:** *I did pretty good despite feeling like I wasn't perfect. The fact is that I did it and this will make me even better the next time I speak.*

By writing down an empowering rebuttal statement in response to the disempowering little voice, you're getting yourself out of a disempowering moment that might sabotage your continued efforts of improving your public speaking.

Again, I emphasize the importance of getting into the habit of writing down rebuttal statements in your empowerment journal. You're building a muscle to nip the disempowering little voices in the bud. Once your muscle is strong, you'll be able to do it on the fly as the little voices show up.

## Trusting Yourself

There is a misconception that trusting yourself is a static disposition within a person, and you either have it in yourself or you don't. It's binary.

I, on the other hand, see trusting yourself like a bank account that you can make deposits into, similar to when you're building trust with a new friend. When you share a personal issue with a friend and they show genuine compassion and empathy, then they just deposited into their trust bank account with you. Over time, this friend accumulates many trust "points" into their trust bank account with you. I see building trust in yourself as following the same principle.

You have a trust bank account with yourself. Each time you set out to do something that's important to you and you do it, you accumulate trust points in your own trust bank account. Each time you do something that you thought you couldn't, you deposit points into your own trust bank account.

After I achieved second place in the World Championship of Public Speaking, my trust within myself sky-rocketed. Not because I thought I was so good, but because then I knew that I could trust myself to work hard, to be determined, and to be stubbornly persistent in doing what I set out to do.

Another example is when I became determined to learn to solve the Rubik's Cube. At first, I mistakenly believed that it was one of those "natural talents" that people had where they picked up the Rubik's Cube and just "figured out" how to solve it.

Then, one day, it dawned on me that solving the Rubik's Cube was just a skill, like playing the piano or public speaking. It has its own mechanics, like learning the scales as part of the mechanics of piano-playing, or learning how to write a speech as part of the mechanics of public speaking. And there are mind skills involved in the Rubik's Cube too, like getting past any limiting self-beliefs and little voices of the inner critic whispering in your ears.

I researched, studied, and got a mentor (my husband) to learn from. I gave myself an hour each night to learn and practice. After a few weeks, I was able to solve the Rubik's Cube. All the while I had to contend with my little voices and limiting self-beliefs, like "It's just too damn hard," "I'm never going to get this," "This is soooooo frustrating," and "Maybe I'm not built for this."

When I finally learned how to solve the darn Rubik's Cube, I deposited many points into my own trust bank account. Again, it was because I knew that I could trust myself to work hard, be determined, be stubbornly persistent, and not let those little voices stop me.

I'm now a speed-cuber, which means I work to lower my time to solve the Rubik's Cube. My current record stands at 1 minute 14 seconds. My next goal is to solve it in under a minute.

What have you always wanted to do or learn, both related to and outside of public speaking? By doing so, you'll deposit major trust points into your own trust bank account. Maybe you can volunteer to give a presentation at work or volunteer to run a workshop for an organization you belong to. You can find opportunities to give a speech outside of work, such as at a local Rotary Club. You can visit a Toastmasters Club in your area and give an impromptu talk.

Perhaps there are things outside of public speaking that you've always wanted to do, like traveling overseas by yourself, learning how to drive a stick shift, learning how to play a song on the piano, or learning to speak a foreign language. If you're intimidated by the mere thought, I suggest you read part III of this book about the process of learning a skill, such as public speaking.

Every time you venture outside your comfort zone, you expand yourself and build more internal trust within yourself. Remember, self-trust is like a bank account that you can deposit into. And you do so by continually challenging yourself to new heights, blasting right through those nagging little voices and limiting self-beliefs.

## Facing Your Fears

I love this quote about fear:

---

# WHAT YOU DON'T FACE STAYS IN YOUR FACE.
### —OTIS WILLIAMS, JR., 1993 WORLD CHAMPION
### OF PUBLIC SPEAKING

---

Another way you can build self-trust points is to face your fears. If you have a fear of giving presentations at work, then you must. If you have a fear of speaking up in a work meeting, then you must. If you are afraid of speaking at a conference in front of hundreds of people, then you must. (In chapter 6, The Process of Mastery, you'll see that you can do so in baby steps. You don't have to throw yourself in the deep end.)

Here are some moments in my life when I faced fears and, in doing so, added significant trust deposits into my internal trust bank account:

- When I pivoted from being a computer programmer to being a software trainer, where I had to speak in front of groups of people, I felt fear and did it anyway.

- When I first gave a speech in front of an association of professional trainers (ASTD—American Society of Training and Development, now called ATD—American Talent Development), I was afraid and did it anyway.
- When I first gave a keynote speech at a conference of several hundred people, I was afraid and did it anyway.
- When I first gave a professional speaking engagement, where an organization paid me to speak, I was afraid and did it anyway.

Facing your fears to build self-trust doesn't have to be just around public speaking. For example, I have a fear of physical confrontation. A contributing factor is that when I was growing up, my older brother practiced karate. When he came home from karate class and learned new moves, guess who he practiced those moves on? Without warning or permission, mind you!

Not that long ago, I decided that I was going to face this fear once and for all, and signed up to learn karate, myself, as an adult. It was very challenging for me to even step in the door of the dojo because I was battling against my fear voices.

I remember the second class I ever attended. I was running a few minutes late from unexpected heavy traffic. When I arrived, the class had already begun. As I approached the dojo room, all I heard were loud shouts of "HEH, HEH, HEH." Very intimidating. So what did I do? In spite of the intimidation, I pushed open the door to participate in the class—I was afraid and did it anyway.

At the time of this writing, I've been taking karate for 18 months. I deposit self-trust points into my bank account when I face my fears around public speaking as well as facing fears outside of public speaking.

What fears can you face that you haven't yet?

Do it. It builds on your self-trust.

## Breaking Through the Myths

There are a number of common misconceptions about public speaking that keep people afraid and disempowered. I'd like to dismantle them and, instead, offer more empowering perspectives on them.

## Myth #1: The Confidence Myth

*The Myth*: I'm waiting for the confidence to come to me, so I can get up and speak in front of a group.

*Another Perspective*: Speak in front of groups, many, many times, and the confidence will come to you—not the other way around.

You might know this truth on an intellectual level. Now I urge you to know it experientially and at a greater level. It's the very act of speaking in front of others over and over again that will increase your confidence. From this vantage point then, I'd encourage you to—**be bold. Go for It. Get up, and speak.**

When I was first learning public speaking, I asked one of my mentors, "How do I become a good speaker?"

He replied, "Mary, the answer is a hundred speeches."

No, I didn't like his response.

He went on to add, "But, Mary, you are asking the wrong question. You should be asking me, 'How do I become a *great* speaker?'"

I responded, "OK, so how do I become a great speaker?"

And guess what he said?

"A thousand speeches."

We don't always have any quantifiable measures that we are moving forward in our momentum of becoming a better speaker. As a result, it can feel like we've stalled or, sometimes, like we're getting worse. So, one way to remind yourself of your progress in a readily-apparent, quantifiable manner is to keep a record of all the times you speak, both formally and less formally.

To serve this purpose, I've created a *Speaker's Log* that you can find as *Worksheet #1* in the *"Present" Yourself in Public Speaking Companion Workbook.* Each time you give a presentation, lead a meeting, give a speech, or get up and share in front of a group, mark it down in the log.

The point here—repetition builds a muscle for the skill AND ends up giving you more confidence. So—be bold. Go for It. Get up, speak, and later record it in your Speaker's Log!

## Myth #2: One-on-One vs. One-to-Many

*The Myth*: Many people tend to view public speaking as a "1:N" activity (one to many). It even appears that way physically to the eyes because you are the **one** person in front of the room while **many** people are in the audience, watching. It's visibly evident. And that's why it feels so scary for many people. It can feel like **one of you** against **many of them** in the crowd.

*Another Perspective*: But there's another way of looking at it. Instead of treating public speaking like it's *one* of you speaking to *many* of them. Reframe it to be **many one-on-one** conversations.

On a practical level, during a speech or presentation, you would make it a point to look at one person and one person only while you say a sentence or two. For those moments, you are only looking at and speaking to that *one* person. Then move your attention on to another person and speak to *them* like they were the only person in the room. By doing so, you're having *many one-on-one* conversations.

This too takes practice, but just merely thinking that you are showing up to have many one-on-one conversations sounds and feels a lot less intimidating than showing up to speak with "a whole bunch" of people.

## Myth #3: I Feel Like a Fraud.

*The Myth*: Feeling like a fraud is a common misconception that the inner critic can whisper to you when it comes to public speaking.

I believe it falls under the umbrella of little voices that stem from the limiting self-belief, "I'm not good enough." You may have heard of the Impostor Syndrome, which is a related phenomenon. I know professional speakers at the top of their fields who still feel like frauds at times (no kidding).

*Another Perspective*: To break away from this self-defeating misconception, I recommend taking this limiting self-belief, "I feel like a fraud," through the 3Rs Process to reframe and release it.

## Myth #4: I'm So Nervous—and the Audience Can Tell.

*The Myth*: The audience can tell how nervous I am, so much that it's making me self-conscious and all I can think about is how nervous I am and how they can tell . . . I'm creating a downward spiral of ever-increasing nervousness and self-consciousness—and it is ruining my ability to give a good speech.

*Another Perspective*: I adopted this concept from one of my mentors, Craig Valentine, the 1999 World Champion of Public Speaking.

The *10x Effect* states: *whatever you're feeling when you're on the stage speaking to an audience, such as nervousness, you feel it 10 times more than the audience can even tell.*

This theory has proved itself true many times in my public speaking classes. During my workshops, I have a participant come to the front of the classroom to speak. Afterwards, I'll ask the person what their experience was like. Many will share, "I was really nervous."

Then I'll turn to the other participants and state, "Raise your hand if you could tell the speaker was nervous." Frequently, no hands go up. And I know they're being honest because I was also sitting in the audience, and many times the speaker looked much more relaxed than they admitted.

I've witnessed the *10x Effect* in practice many, many times in my classes to know that it applies in most cases.

So the next time you feel nervous in front of a room, remember that you're most likely feeling it 10 times more than the audience can tell.

## Myth #5: The Audience Is Judging Me.

*The Myth*: I feel like I'm being judged by the audience.

*Another Perspective*: Here is another piece of news that should offer you some relief: the people in your audience are tuned into one radio station, WIIFM. It stands for "What's in it for me?"

Why is this a relief? Because you no longer need to be concerned about what people in your audience think of you or how they are judging you—because they're most likely not even thinking about you. Who are they thinking and caring about? Themselves. They don't really care about you. They're just looking to get some benefits for themselves from what you're saying. For example, they might be thinking:

- How can what you're saying help me?
- How does what you're saying apply to me?
- What can I take away from your presentation that I can use in my life/work/home?

So while "they don't really care about you" may sound harsh, it's actually very liberating for the speaker because you realize where the audience's focus is, on themselves, so they aren't busy judging you.

## Myth #6: It's ALL about Me.

*The Myth*: Your primary concerns are about you. Your focus is all about you.

You—how you look, feel, talk, make eye contact, connect to the audience, forget words—you are what is so important about your public speaking.

*Another Perspective*: It's NOT about you! You are there to serve your audience (inspire, entertain, inform, etc). So—it's really all about THEM.

If I was to put the voice inside of your head on loud-speaker just before you're about to give a presentation, it might sound like this:

*I'm nervous. I feel like I haven't prepared enough. Will they like what I say? Am I gonna stuff up? I hope I don't forget anything. Am I gonna look good? Am I gonna make a fool out of myself? Is my boss gonna think I did a good job? Is my boss gonna be judging me? Am I gonna to sound like an idiot?*

When I illustrate the above to my students, I'm commonly met with giggles and they tell me they can relate. If you were to analyze the above scenario, who is the primary focus on? Me, me, me, and me (the speaker).

Let me further explain with a personal story. Leading up to my World Championship finals, my main concern was that I was running out of time. The contest date was only one week away, and my speech was still flat and uninspiring.

I felt as though I was part-way through completing a jigsaw puzzle with a thousand pieces, and I lost the lid to the box. I felt lost. I'd forgotten the overall picture of why I was doing it. At this point I'd been practicing for six months straight. I'd sacrificed my social life and anything fun. I felt like quitting but dragged myself to yet another rehearsal for a group of 50 interns at a large bank. I gave my speech, and it was just OK.

That afternoon, I got home exhausted. I felt like my mental, emotional, and physical energy had been wrung dry. I thought, "Mary, why are you putting yourself through this torture?"

I didn't even have the energy to look through the feedback sheets, and I had another rehearsal scheduled the next morning. I forced myself to look at the feedback anyway, and I came across this from a young intern from my audience:

*Mary, I learned a lot from your speech. You pointed out my major problem, my inner critic. I never saw that before. Thank you.*

That's when I "found my lid." It hit me like a ton of bricks—*it's **not** about me*. I was there to serve and inspire my audience. Instead, I'd been focused on how "**I'm** exhausted, **I** want my free time, **I** don't want to work anymore. Me, me, me, me, me, me." It had become all about me.

Moments before a presentation or speech, what concerns or worries come up for you? When I poll my workshop participants with the same question, here are some typical concerns they share:

- *What if I might go blank?*
- *What if I sound stupid?*
- *I might have spinach in my teeth.*
- *I'm so nervous. I'm sure they can tell.*
- *Will they remember my speech? Or will it be a waste of time?*
- *The fact-checkers will tell me I'm wrong.*
- *I need to hit all my points and do it in time.*
- *What if I mispronounce words?*

Notice these concerns are all about "me" and "I." When you're a speaker and you focus on yourself, there's only a certain level of effectiveness that you can reach before you hit a ceiling.

However, by focusing on serving your audience, then you can take it to a whole other level. This requires you to let go of your own insecurities and the inner critic's little voices. In essence, you need to "get over yourself," which is what this whole book is about. To help you do just that.

The next time you speak on the stage, ask yourself, "Is it going to be about me? Or is it going to be about my audience?"

## Myth #7: He or she hates me.

*The Myth*: When speaking in front of an audience, many people get intimidated or "put off" by the non-verbal signs that a person in the audience might be giving off. For example, the man in the third row yawns, so you think, "I must be boring." Or the woman in the second row looks at her watch, so you think, "She can't wait to get out of here."

*Another Perspective*: This is when "Notice, Don't Interpret" can be very helpful for the public speaker. I learned this from master Story Theater Method coach, Doug Stevenson. I've since found having this "Notice, Don't interpret" tool in my back pocket to be very handy. Let me explain how it works.

In one of my first professional speaking gigs, a public speaking workshop for 50 engineers, the workshop was going well, and people were engaged and participating in interactive discussions.

That's when I saw her. In the front row, sat a woman wearing a bright green jacket. Throughout the entire workshop, she looked at me with a sour expression on her face as if to say, "I hate every word you're saying." Each time I looked at this angry-looking woman, the little voice in my head explained, "Oh my gosh, she's silently heckling me," and that thought would suck a bit of energy from me.

At the end of the two-hour workshop, this same woman came running up to my table where I had my educational items displayed and exclaimed, "Mary, I want to buy all of your CDs. Everything you said resonated with me."

WHAT? I couldn't believe what she was saying. This was the woman who sat there the entire time, looking at me with a grumpy frown and what I thought was total disapproval. That's when I finally got what Doug Stevenson was saying: notice, don't interpret.

I had been noticing her grouchy expression and interpreted it to mean that she was displeased with what I was saying. In reality, that wasn't what she was thinking. For all I know that's what her face looks like when she is concentrating, but I had been interpreting it to mean the worst. I allowed my little voice to do the interpretation.

When you're speaking in front of an audience and there is a person looking at you in an odd way, simply notice, but don't interpret.

## Myth #8: I Need to Be Perfect.

*The Myth*: One of the most commonly held limiting self-beliefs that I've witnessed from many of my students is the unconscious need to be perfect. They put an enormous amount of pressure on themselves to be perfect, and when they don't perform to the level in their minds that constitutes "perfection," they beat themselves up over it. This is a trap. I know this trap as well as anyone.

When I first pivoted from being a computer programmer to a trainer, I worked really hard to learn the material. I practiced it, rehearsed with my colleagues, got feedback, and even attended train-the-trainer courses. I was fully prepared.

On the morning of my first "real" training gig in front of the company's highly-valued client, I called my training manager who was an amazing coach and mentor.

"Jerry, I'm so nervous," I admitted.

Jerry asked me a question, "Mary, what is your main concern?"

I immediately responded, "I don't want to make a mistake."

What Jerry said next has stayed with me all these years. It's affected every presentation and training that I've ever done since. "Mary, here's what I want you to do. Go out there and make at least three mistakes. And after the training I want you to come back and report the mistakes to me. If you don't have at least three mistakes, don't even bother to call me because I won't accept your call."

I gasped and then I laughed because I realized what she was doing. Jerry gave me "permission" to make mistakes. By making mistakes mandatory, she helped to downgrade the significance of a "mistake" in my mind.

In reality, I knew the training material very well, and if anything did come up in the training that I didn't know, I was professional enough to handle it and find out for the client later on.

*Another Perspective*: No one wants or expects you to be perfect. They want you to be real and to help them. We'll talk a lot more about this in the next chapter entitled Being Real.

Give yourself space to make mistakes. Perfectionism is an ideal that no human being can reach. Why set such unattainable standards for yourself? It will just cause you stress and anxiety.

## Self-Belief and the Growth Mindset

One day after class, a student, Sue, approached me and confided, "Mary, I have trouble believing in myself. When I see other people who speak confidently, I wish I spoke with such belief and conviction. Do you have any advice about how I can believe in myself more?"

We've all experienced the little voice of self-doubt, especially if we are outside our comfort zone. But belief is more fundamental. It's the container in which we hold our learning.

Self-belief is an inner conviction that if you put in the work, you will acquire the skill. Carol Dweck, PhD, professor of psychology at Stanford University and author of the bestselling book *Mindset: The New Psychology of Success*, refers to this kind of attitude as a "growth mindset." Compare the growth mindset to that of someone with a fixed mindset who believes that they're either good at something or they're not.

Self-belief is difficult if you have a fixed mindset. The good news—you can change your mindset. In chapter 6, The Process of Mastery, we'll delve into the growth mindset vs. the fixed mindset by examining Dr. Dweck's research. For now, I encourage you to adopt a growth mindset.

## Borrowing Belief

To answer Sue's question, I reflected on my own journey and what I did to boost my own belief in myself along the way. Then I replied, "Sue, here's what I want you to do. *Borrow* a belief." Because she looked puzzled, I explained it to her this way:

When I first joined Toastmasters and gave my second-ever speech, I was very self-conscious and self-judgmental. After my speech, the club president, Chai, a very confident young lady, came up to me and stated, "Mary, I see something in you. You might not see it in yourself yet, but one day, you'll be a very good speaker."

I had no idea what she saw, and I certainly didn't believe it about myself. But I believed that *she* believed it—so I *borrowed* her belief. I began operating on borrowed belief.

Four years later, I gave a speech at a district conference. Afterwards, the past district governor named Bash Turay, a very distinguished gentleman, wearing a suit and tie, came up to me (I'd never met him in person) and said, "Mary, you're good. You could be on the World Championship's stage." I was flabbergasted by his comment. He must have seen the bewildered look on my face, so he continued, "Really, Mary, you're *that* good".

In that moment, I didn't believe that about myself, but I believed that *he* believed it. I thought, "Here is someone who has been to and witnessed many World Championships. If *he* believes that I'm good, then I'm sure as heck going to *borrow* his belief."

So if you find it challenging to believe in yourself, listen to the people in your life who believe in you and believe *them.* **Borrow** their belief like I did. Little by little, the belief will become your own. And if you already believe in yourself, congratulations. You can use other people's belief in you to reinforce that belief in yourself.

Self-belief is like a muscle. Once it's strong enough, it can lift the weight of your self-doubts that may and probably will arise periodically, especially when you're outside your comfort zone.

## Environment

I encourage you to find an environment that values progression, one where you're surrounded by people who support and encourage you and value what you're up to. Don't underestimate the power of this suggestion. You want the people around you to reflect back to you the most positive version of yourself.

The corollary of that is stay the heck away from naysayers because energy is contagious. Have you ever been having a good day and then you talk to someone who points out all the "faults" in your speech or in what you're doing but has no suggestions on how to improve it? The next thing you know, you feel drained of energy? I call these people "energy vampires" because they just "suck" the energy right out of you.

You really must find people and communities that support what you're up to, people who are also in the process of improving their own public speaking and communication skills. I highly recommend Toastmasters International, National Speaker's Association, and Association for Talent Development (formerly ASTD, American Society of Training and Development).

## The Changing of Your "States"

You could be doing a million things right now, but you're not. You're here, reading this book. You want to learn and grow. I have no doubt in my mind that you're motivated. So the question isn't "*Are* you motivated?" The question is "How do you to *stay* motivated?"

In walking the path to become a better public speaker, sometimes you fall out of motivation and become disenchanted with the process. It's at these times when you'll need to know how to re-motivate yourself to get back on the path.

At any given moment, you are in a particular "state." For example, your state may be calm, motivated, lazy, overwhelmed, contemplative, focused, etc. Be mindful of what state you're in, and if you find yourself in a sub-optimal state, like you are feeling anxious just before a presentation, then you can proactively shift your own state.

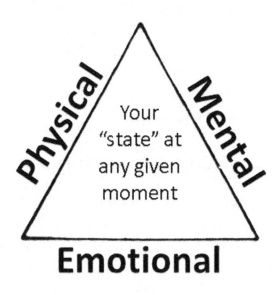

The above diagram, representing your state at any given moment, is comprised of three sides:

1. Physical—your body and its movements
2. Mental—your mental world of thoughts
3. Emotional—how you feel emotionally

## Change Your State

All three sides of the triangle are linked. This means that if you shift one side, the other two sides also shift.

## Changing the Physical Side

What do you think is the quickest side to shift? In my experience, I would say the physical side. For example:

- Take a walk.
- Go for a run.
- Go to the gym.

During my World Championship of Public Speaking journey, I ran almost every day to keep my energy up and stay motivated. So when you're feeling down, change your physical state and you'll have altered your overall state.

## Changing the Mental Side

Getting out of your head to change the mental state is a little more challenging. Because you need to snap out of the thoughts in the first place, become aware of what you're thinking and consciously choose new thoughts. And it *can* be done. Here are some ways to change your mental state:

- Call a friend.
- Post inspiring quotes around you, so you can have them handy to read when you need them. Quotes are a fast way to become conscious of an empowering thought, thereby snapping you out of a disempowering state of mind.
- Write in your LVJ (little voice journal).
- Read your empowerment journal.

## Changing the Emotional Side

Finally, you can change your state by changing your emotions. What are some of the ways you can change your emotional state? Here are some examples I use in my life, some of which I drew from my students:

- Listen to music that motivates you.
- Write poetry.
- Watch your favorite stand-up comedians on YouTube.
- Watch your favorite movie.
- Hug someone—your partner, your kids, a good friend, your dog.

## The Power of Changing Your State in Public Speaking

You can consciously change your state just before a presentation or any time along your public speaking journey when you feel disenchanted with the process. In this way you retake control and put yourself back "in state" to continue your public speaking growth.

## A Word about Emotions

There's no shame in feeling. Our culture tends to abhor feeling, like it's a bad thing. You hear phrases, like "Oh, that's so touchy-feely." I submit to you a different point of view. To be human is to feel. Sometimes we forget that and unconsciously bottle up our feelings or sweep them under the rug. I, of all people, ought to know about this.

I grew up with a dad who was an engineer, a very linear thinker. He was very practical. His philosophy was "If you can't see it, it doesn't exist" and "Quit your whining and man up." As a child, I basically learned:

---

### BRAIN IS GOOD. INTELLECTUAL, GOOD. FEELINGS—WHAT'S THAT?

---

So sometimes when I have trouble releasing my feelings that are strong and I feel blocked, I use music to help me feel and release. If I'm feeling sad and I'm having trouble releasing it, I will listen to sad music or watch a sad movie to help bring it out. I might even have a private crying session, all by myself, no holds bar and no judgment. It's just a release. And that brings me back to equilibrium.

You can do the same.

To continue along your journey to become a better public speaker, I encourage you to change either your physical, mental, or emotional state to alter your overall state to one of self-motivation.

## CHAPTER 3 GOLDEN NUGGETS

This chapter was all about setting yourself up to win. Win in what? Win in supporting yourself to be in the optimal mindset to execute your goal of becoming a better public speaker.

- The disempowering little voices in your head are the voices of your inner critic.
- When you slip into feeling bad about yourself or your public speaking progress, use it as an opportunity to catch what the little voices are saying.
- Objectively look at any underlying limiting self-beliefs using the 3Rs Process of *reflection, recall,* and *reframe.*
- Challenge those limiting self-beliefs you developed at some point in your past.

I took you through some very practical ways of empowering yourself that I've implemented in my life.

- Create a little voice journal (LVG) and an empowerment journal to record the criticism that you observe from the inner critic and next to offset the criticism with an empowering thought (what would your best friend say?).

- Self-trust is like a bank account: you need to deposit into it regularly by doing what you thought you couldn't, like volunteering to give a presentation and facing your fears by stepping out of your comfort zone a little at a time.

- There are some common misconceptions that keep many people in fear of public speaking. Remember, when your inner critic suggests scary myths, you can regain your power by engaging with the alternative, constructive perspectives of the myths.

- Believing in yourself can be enhanced by *borrowing* beliefs from others who believe in you until you can stand in your own belief of yourself.

- Surround yourself with people who are on the path to become better public speakers and communicators. This will help to accelerate your own growth as a public speaker.

- At any given moment be aware of your state. If you are in a sub-optimal state, consciously shift your physical, mental, or emotional state to achieve a more productive state.

# CHAPTER 4

# BEING REAL

After you've set yourself up to come from an empowering context, the next part of the inside-out approach is becoming real. This chapter is about embracing who you really are at your core, so you can be real with any audience. Authenticity is a direct gateway to connection.

This means working on taking off the "masks" and connecting with who you are underneath—in full acceptance of yourself. This means taking off the burden of self-consciousness, like a heavy overcoat, to set yourself free as a public speaker. In order to be liberated to just be yourself on the platform, you must let go of barriers, such as your ego, that prevent you from just being your wonderful self.

Legendary professional public speaker Bill Gove observed:

# IF I WANT TO BE FREE, I'VE GOT TO BE ME. I BETTER KNOW WHO ME IS.

And that's the essence of this chapter: to help you explore, discover, and connect with who you are authentically so that you align yourself with that for your audience, fully self-expressed and proud of what you represent for them.

As human beings living in society, I've observed that it's common to become numb to who we are and what values we stand for. Social conditioning and many rules bombard us before we even have a chance to become clear on who we are. As a result, many of us are not aligned with what makes our spirit come alive and, therefore, feel disconnected from ourselves. If you're disconnected from yourself, how on earth can you connect with your audience in any genuine way?

You're not trying to be perfect. You're taking the pressure off, so you can be real, and that means removing barriers to authenticity, like your ego and self-consciousness.

# Authenticity

To be authentic means to be real. You're no longer afraid to let them see who you really are, warts 'n all. In other words, you are who you are, you aren't who you're not, and you're good with that. How liberating is that?

When I first started to learn public speaking, I took my mentor's advice, video-taped myself, and watched the recording with the volume muted. With only the visual of my presentation and no sound to distract me, I saw exactly how serious I looked. I never smiled once. From that moment, I knew I needed to lighten up. There was a disconnect between who I was in real life (open, friendly, silly) to who I was being on stage (stiff, serious, and uptight).

Bridging that gap wasn't easy, and it didn't happen overnight. I needed to remove my barriers to being real. I learned how to do this—and now, I'm going to guide you through how to do it too.

## Your Highest Values

What are your highest values?

Here's an exercise I recommend. Spend 3 to 5 minutes brainstorming words or short phrases that resonate with what you're about. For example, you could reflect on the question, "What are your highest intentions?" Don't filter your answers. From this list you brainstormed, narrow it down to a short list of about a dozen words that most resonate with you.

For example, my short list includes:

- *Empowerment*
- *Adding value*
- *Love*
- *Light*
- *Healing*
- *Awaken*
- *Living my truth*
- *Authenticity*
- *Expression*
- *Laughter*
- *Fun*
- *Peace*
- *Service*
- *Become wiser*
- *Joy*

## Your Intention Chart

Get a large piece of blank paper and write in huge letters, "What is my intention?" Then around this question, write your short list of words. Decorate this sheet of paper using colors, drawing little pictures, or whatever makes you feel good.

This is your intention chart. The words on it represent your highest intentions. Take a photo of your intention chart with your smart phone and carry a copy of it around with you. When preparing for a presentation, right beforehand, look at your intention chart and become present to the words you wrote. Consciously come from these values as you're speaking to your audience.

If you come from this place of your highest intention for the audience, you will less likely be focused on yourself. This is being authentic to what you stand for—your highest values and intentions.

## Courage to Be Vulnerable

A part of being authentic is embracing being vulnerable and coming from the heart. It takes courage to be vulnerable in front of an audience. Some of us don't even want to admit vulnerability, let alone in front of an audience. It also takes courage to come from your heart, especially on stage.

The origin of the word "courage" comes from French words, "coeur," meaning "heart," and "âge," meaning the length of existence measured in time. So "courage" really means a time for the heart.

## COEUR—ÂGE = A TIME FOR THE HEART

Do you have heart in your speeches and presentations?

People are not purely persuaded through logic. Their emotions are also strong drivers. When you have heart and the audience feels it, they're more likely to *buy into* what you're saying. Story Theater coach Doug Stevenson says it best: "Emotion is the fast lane to the brain." Have courage to show emotion on stage when it's appropriate.

Before I started speaking professionally, I attended a talk by a very successful professional speaker. While he gave us a lot of good information, I sat wondering if I could reproduce his success in this arena because he was speaking from his current vantage point of where he was at that moment.

An audience member asked him what it was like when he first started out as a professional speaker. He then spoke about the initial challenges and struggles he went through. Immediately, he became relatable to me because his stories gave me the hope that if he could do it despite his challenges, then maybe I could too.

The moral of the story is—don't be so set on projecting an invulnerable persona of yourself for your audience. Paradoxically, it's when you reveal your struggles and how you overcame them that you become more relatable to the audience.

## Sincerity

There's a saying, "They don't care how much you know until they know how much you care." When someone is speaking, sincerity is a quality of earnestness that conveys a person is genuine. It carries with it a sense of trust.

I've witnessed presentations and speeches that were not particularly well-organized and the quality of the information was only OK, but the tone of the presenter was sincere and, therefore, had an impact on the audience.

On the other hand, if I doubt a speaker's sincerity, the speech won't come across as powerfully even if the information is spot-on.

When I see a speaker who is sincere, I feel a level of genuine caring and concern that they have about the topic they're speaking about. They just seem real and, therefore, more believable and convincing.

Work on being sincere. And how do you do that? You come from a space of "It's not about me"—it's about helping my audience. And you become aware of barriers that might be in the way.

## Barriers to Authenticity

To be authentic, we must be aware of the potential barriers that stand in the way of our being real. I'm going to specify some of those barriers.

### Big Barrier 1—The Ego

Your ego is interested in two things: to look good and avoid looking bad.

Human beings have egos. It's a part of being human. It's not inherently a bad thing. But if you allow your ego to be the main driver on the platform, the *real* you who represents your highest values becomes opaque to the audience and impact is lost in the exchange.

Your audience prefers to see and hear from the real you, not your ego.

## Big Barrier 2—The Fear of Not Knowing the Answer

"I hate the Q and A period." I hear this time and time again from my workshop participants. When I ask them why, the answer is always the same: "Because I don't like it when they ask me a question I don't know the answer to."

Here is a typical exchange on this topic as it happens in one of my workshops:

**Mary**: Let's pause right there. What's the problem here? Why don't you like it? Why is it such a big deal not to know the answer to a question?

**Participant**: I don't want to look stupid.

**Mary**: Ah-ha. So it's the fear of looking bad.

**Participant**: Yes, exactly.

Here's some good news: no one expects you to know everything under the sun. As a human being, it's not even possible. So really, you're afraid they're going to find out that you're human, which, by the way, you are. Just in case you think you're not. So, sorry to break that news to you.

## Suggested Solutions for Fear of the Q and A Period

*Some Appropriate Professional Responses*

You've been asked a question you don't know the answer to. What are some appropriate responses?

Here are some tricks that I learned as a trainer for when the scenario occurs. I've used these techniques over and over again, and no one has ever said, "That's unacceptable."

- "That's a great question. I don't know from the top of my head. Let me get back to you on that." And make sure you find out the answer afterwards and get back to them.
- "That's a great question. Does anyone else in the room know?" Almost always, someone in the room has the answer or at least an insightful point to make about it. The person just wants "an" answer, and it doesn't have to come from you. When you're in front of the room, you're a facilitator as much as a presenter. You can facilitate the group to come up with the answer if appropriate.
- Depending on the situation, you might be able to find the answer online right there on the spot. I've given many training classes where I didn't know the answer to a question,

and I've said, "Wait one minute, let me look that up for you." Then I hop on the laptop, find the answer online, and take care of it in that moment.

*Build a Bucket List*

Carmine Gallo, author of *The Presentation Secrets of Steve Jobs*, suggests preparing beforehand a bucket list of possible difficult questions your audience might ask in the Q and A. Include the "scary" questions. For each question, research and prepare an answer. In this way, by making the unknown known to you, you minimize fear of the unknown.

I've built and used a bucket list in my trainings, and it has paid dividends many times over.

## Big Barrier 3—Denying Your "Shadow"

Real people have dark sides. To deny that fact is to deny being human. You're better off acknowledging your dark side and understanding it. Chances are, you're probably already aware of the darker sides of yourself.

During your speech, if you reveal hints of your darker side, your "shadow," the audience can better connect with you because it makes you sound real, just like they are. Talking about your lower-self doesn't have to be heavy; it can be light and tongue-in-cheek.

The late Debbie Ford's teachings broadened my understanding of the dark side of my own nature. Her book *The Dark Side of the Light Chasers* helped me to see that not only is it normal but useful for me to have a dark side.

For example, one of my "shadows" is I can be annoyingly bossy. One time during a software training gig to a client corporation, a C-level executive in the audience became visibly agitated and exclaimed angrily, "Why was it done this way?"

My shadow kicked in and bossily replied, "Because your team made the decision that way!" And then I added, "We can always look into changing it later on if the team agrees." He backed down, and I regained composure and control of the class.

Your "shadow" can be useful if you channel it productively. Acknowledging it and accepting it removes it as a barrier to your authentic self. It's a part of you. Denying that you have a darker side is rejecting a part of yourself. That's not being authentic to who you are.

## Big Barrier 4—Taking Yourself Too Seriously

Real people laugh at times. Being able to laugh at yourself takes the pressure off, and you can be more relaxed on stage. If you can laugh at yourself, you give your audience permission to laugh and relax also.

There's a myth that presentations and speeches, especially those done in a business setting, need to be serious and stuffy. Nothing can be further from the truth.

I've spoken to many business audiences, and no one has ever come up to me to complain that I should've been more serious. Why? Because laughing is fun. Laughing implies that you're enjoying yourself. And who doesn't want to enjoy themselves? Especially in a business setting where most presentations *are* serious and, let's face it, dry and boring?

Don't take yourself so seriously. Have fun with it. :-)

## Big Barrier 5—The Curse of Self-Consciousness

Recently, I was listening to Tim Ferriss's podcast where he interviewed the talented movie actor, Ed Norton. Ed talked about how as soon as a camera is on you, there's a tendency to act differently than you would if nobody was watching. This phenomenon is called self-consciousness.

When you're speaking in front of the room, many eyes are looking at you. That's not an everyday occurrence for most people. You don't have **that** many eyes on you at one time usually. In fact, most of us aren't used to having even one pair of eyes on us for any lengthy period of time. And here you are, on stage being looked at by people for a prolonged period of time. It can feel very unnatural and spin you into self-consciousness.

Practice becoming aware of catching yourself when you feel self-conscious, and let it go because it can be a barrier to being your authentic self, both on and off the platform.

### Big Barrier 6—Eye Contact Is Scary

I noticed something that my students were telling me, over and over again, regardless of their profession, age, gender, or nationality:

---

## EYE CONTACT IS SCARY.

---

When I reflected on my own experience, I instinctively understood what they were saying.

If you're unsure, you can do this as an experiment. On a weekday, during peak time, around 8 am, on public transport, look at someone sitting across from you and observe their reaction. When they notice you're looking at them, they'll likely look away quickly and uncomfortably. I'm not encouraging you to be creepy and stare at people but to simply be aware that looking at someone can make them and you feel uncomfortable.

Easier said than done though, isn't it? Here are two suggestions that you can adopt to "train" yourself to be less self-conscious when being "looked at" and to get over the scariness of it.

- *Notice what comes up*—Look at this scariness directly in the eye (pun intended). When speaking with an audience and you feel self-conscious (scary/weird/awkward), be honest with yourself and observe what your little voices are saying to you. After your presentation, write them down in your LVJ (little voice journal). Again, you can use *Worksheet #6: Little Voice/Empowerment Journal* in your companion workbook.

In my experience leading my students through this very practice, it's common that when we peel back the layers, a limiting self-belief is uncovered. For example, a student in my class asked me, "I find eye contact to be scary. How can I get over that?"

I responded by offering her an opportunity to practice eye contact in front of the class. "For one minute, just look at people in the audience without saying anything." Her eyes bulged out of her head as if to say, "What?"

I continued, "Pause, right there—what is your little voice saying right now?"

Her immediate reply was "Oh shit!"

Everyone laughed.

When I guided her to peel back the layers, she "saw" that what she was afraid of was being "found out." The limiting self-belief that the situation triggered in her was "What if I'm not good enough?"

Once you've identified what that limiting self-belief is, you can run it through the 3Rs Process that we talked about in chapter 3 to reframe that limitation in an empowering way—and then release it.

- *Practice being "looked at" by creating a "pretend" audience*—Many years ago, I learned this technique from speaking coach Carla Kimball. What you do is cut out large photos of people's faces from magazines and stick them on chairs to build an "audience." You then practice speaking in front of your "audience," all in the privacy of your own home. This might sound odd, but you'd be surprised that although these are not "real" people, the eyes looking at you can and do trigger the same little voices in your head that actual human beings do. As one of my mentors used to say to me, "Don't knock it until you try it." Don't take my word for it, try this out for yourself.

# CHAPTER 4 GOLDEN NUGGETS

Ironically, it's difficult to be yourself on the platform when you're public speaking. This is because of a few reasons:

- One, it's not every day that you are being "looked at" by so many others.
- And secondly, you may not have taken the time to align yourself with who you are and what you stand for.

Once you're aware of what your highest values are:

- It's easier to be authentically you because the intention of your presentation can come from those values.
- It becomes less important to you what you "look like" during your speech (which is ego and fear-driven).
- What becomes more important is that you're sincere and courageously vulnerable to be you.

Again, it's not easy to be authentic. You must look at what makes it difficult (the common barriers) that keep you a prisoner of "the masks" you wear to hide who you really are:

- Ego
- Fear
- Denying parts of yourself
- Taking yourself too seriously
- And, of course, self-consciousness

It's not about being perfect, it's about being real. Being real is a form of freedom because you don't have to pretend. Pretending takes an enormous amount of energy. To be real means embracing who you are, all sides of you.

When you can be real with people, your sincerity comes through and you will have a far greater impact on your audience. The better you are at being you, the less pressure there is to "perform," the more relaxed you'll be, and the more fun you—and your audience—will have as a result.

# CHAPTER 5

# PRESENCE

You've now thought about your highest values, learned about taking off your "masks" to be more real, and are aware of the barriers to being authentically you. Now it's time to take the experience of being clear and open on the platform to the next level. In this chapter we explore what stage presence means. You'll find that presence means being in the now, not lost in thoughts and the murmurings of the little voices.

We'll explore stage presence and what can distract you from being present while on the platform. I'll also show you a formula to follow to get back into presence when you notice that you are not. We look at the science behind why practicing being mindful helps you to be present. The neuroscience of how the mind works reveals a lot about why the mind wanders, especially before and during a presentation.

By understanding and practicing stage presence, this chapter shows you how to maintain presence on the stage.

## What Is Stage Presence?

Think of someone who has stage presence. What word comes to mind to describe this stage presence? There's no right or wrong answer. When I ask my workshop participants this same question, here are some common answers that I hear:

- *Confidence*
- *Performance*
- *Recognition*
- *Attention*
- *Electricity*
- *Charisma*
- *Comfort*
- *Communication*

*Now I'd like you to think about the word presence.* Think about what that word means.

The word *presence* comes from the word *present*. To be *present* means to *be in the moment*. In other words, stage presence simply means being in the moment on stage. So, in public speaking, it means being in the moment when you are speaking with an audience.

## Being in the Moment

Picture a timeline, like the one below. If the middle of the timeline represents *present*, what would the left and right ends of the timeline represent?

←——— ??? ——————— Present ——————— ??? ———→

The answer: the past and future.

←——— Past ——————— Present ——————— Future ———→

So *present* and *being in the moment* really mean *being here, right now*. Not yesterday, not tomorrow, not one second ago, and not one second from now.

Right now!

## What Does *Being in the Moment* Mean in Public Speaking?

While public speaking, you are physically on the stage, but, for many people, their mind is somewhere else, lost in thought, especially if they're not used to being on stage. That's not being present.

So when you're not being present, what's happening to your mind? Your focus is being hijacked by racing thoughts, bouncing back and forth, like a ball in a pinball machine. You are being distracted.

What distracts you from being in the present moment when you're speaking on stage? What distracts you from being in the now? Again, there's no right or wrong. When I ask this question of my workshop participants, here are some common responses I hear:

- *Outside noise and glare*
- *My mental clutter*
- *The mistake I just made*
- *What I'm supposed to say next*
- *Time pressures*
- *When I feel like I'm not connecting with my audience*
- *When I'm lost in thought*
- *My pants are too tight. The waistline is digging into my belly.*

## Three Categories of Distractions

We can summarize all the distractions that take us away from the present moment into three categories: thoughts (mental world), feelings (emotional world), and body and environment (physical world).

Remember in the previous chapter, we looked at the triangle of "states" and how your state at any given moment is comprised of three sides—the mental, emotional, and physical? The three categories of fall into the same three mediums. That's not a coincidence. Let me explain: as a human being, your experiences in aggregate come from your mental world of thoughts, emotional world of feelings, and the physical world of the body.

In chapter 3 we talked about how turning the knobs of any of these sides, the physical, mental, or emotional, would change your overall state. Here we see this parallel in that can come in any form from any of the three sides, a distraction from a thought (mental), a distraction from an emotion, or a physical distraction.

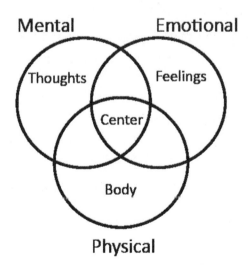

3 Categories of Distractions

Mental     Emotional

Thoughts     Feelings

Center

Body

Physical

## Distraction Type 1—Thought (Mental World)

There are three types of thought that are commonly experienced while public speaking that may distract you from being in the present.

*The First: Empowering Thoughts*

Empowering thoughts empower you while you're on stage. For example:

- *I'm doing great.*
- *I prepared well.*
- *The audience is really connected with me.*

*The Second: Disempowering Thoughts*

Where there are empowering thoughts, there are disempowering thoughts too. The disempowering thoughts stem from the little voice of your inner critic taking you away from being in the moment. For example:

- *I'm not prepared.*
- *That man in the front row is looking at his watch. I must be boring.*
- *I can't wait until this is over. I feel so self-conscious.*

*The Third: Neutral Thoughts*

These are thoughts that are neither empowering nor disempowering. For example:

- *That lady is wearing a lovely necklace.*
- *There are some bright lights in the back.*
- *The data projector is mounted on the ceiling. That's interesting.*

## Distraction Type 2—Feelings (Emotional World)

Like it or not, you're a human being, not an automaton. You do experience feelings and emotions while you're speaking on stage. There are many types of emotions. In David Brooks's book, *The Seven Strategies of Master Presenters*, he summarizes emotions into six basic types:

1. Happiness
2. Sadness
3. Fear
4. Anger
5. Surprise
6. Disgust

No matter what country you're from, whether you're male or female, you've experienced these emotions at one time or another.

Even if you don't speak the same language, it's often obvious to know what emotion someone is feeling. For example, if someone approaches you speaking in French and you don't understand French, but they're yelling at you with their eyes wide open and veins popping out from their forehead, it's a safe bet they're angry.

And when an emotion is happening within you on the stage, it takes self-awareness to "see" the emotion as it's happening internally. And that can distract us from being in the moment, especially if the emotion is strong.

For example, if you don't feel prepared and are anxious as you're speaking, you are feeling the basic emotion of fear.

### Distraction Type 3—Body and Environment (Physical World)

What elements from the physical world can keep us from being in the present moment when public speaking? When I ask my students this same question, here are some common responses:

- *Pain*—one time before a presentation, I had severe heart burn.
- *Illness*—having a cold and sinuses during a talk.

- *Wardrobe malfunction*—a button pops.
- *Physical discomfort*—you ate too much before the presentation, and now your pants feel too tight because the waistline is digging into your stomach.
- *Hunger*
- *Thirst*
- *Tired*
- *Sleepiness*
- *Air conditioning is too loud.*
- *The room is stuffy and hot.*
- *There's a large column between you and a section of the audience.*

These physical  can keep you from being in the moment when speaking on stage.

## Calming Yourself before Going on Stage

Now that we've looked at what distracts us from being in the present, how do we get in the moment and be calm on stage? That's the tricky part, isn't it?

In the context of the diagram above, that area in the middle where the three circles intersect represents presence—a space where you're undistracted.

## PRESENCE = CLEAR FROM THOUGHT + CLEAR FROM EMOTION + FREE FROM PHYSICAL DISTRACTIONS

Below are some recommendations and practice exercises for becoming present:

### 1. Release the Adrenalin

Before you go on stage to speak, you can release excess adrenalin by getting physical. Move your body—jump up and down (at the back of the room or in the hallway, not on stage) or go for a short walk just before your presentation.

One of my mentors, Mark Brown, has been known to do push-ups before getting on stage to release some of that adrenalin and calm himself.

### 2. Get Still

An analogy that I love to describe this process is a snow globe. Imagine you just shook up a snow globe, and the snow flakes are bouncing rapidly everywhere within it. The internal environment of your mind is just like that snow globe with many thoughts and emotions bouncing around. You feel unsettled. Your internal world is being very disruptive to your attention.

When you take time to get still, perhaps by following your breath, you're taking your snow globe and placing it down on the table, thus allowing the snow flakes to settle to the bottom, so your internal landscape comes to stillness—clear of thought, clear of emotion, free from physical distraction. Re-centering your attention brings you back to presence.

In the next section I give you exercises to practice getting still.

## 3. Get Clear on Your Intentions

Have your intention chart that you created in chapter 3 with you, and read it to re-presence yourself to your highest intentions.

You can even create an intention statement. For example, before a presentation or training class, I write down my intention statement, which is "My intention is to empower individuals, both personally and professionally."

## Practice Getting Still—Using Your Breath as an Anchor

Practicing breathing does not sound like a big deal. But when you're about to speak in public and you're lost in thoughts of fear and anxiety, the ability to come back to presence using a few seconds of focused breathing *is* a big deal because that's when you need to come right back to calm and presence. That's why it's called an anchor—it pulls you back and prevents your boat of thoughts and emotions from drifting away.

The concept of practicing breathing might even sound weird. Don't we breathe all the time? Automatically? Why do we have to practice that? Yes, we're breathing all the time, but we're not always *conscious* that we're breathing.

**The Exercise**

Here's a simple breathing exercise that I lead my students through in workshops. It takes less than a minute to do.

Just for one minute, do the following:

1. Take a slow deep breath through your nose for a count of six.
2. Notice that little space of transition from in-breath to out-breath.
3. Breathe out through your nose slowly for a count of six, feeling your shoulders and body relax.

Feel free to close your eyes or keep them open. As you get used to doing the above exercise, you might like to add a mantra statement to say in your head, such as "I am here right now."

After this exercise, check in with yourself, asking, "How do I feel?" Repeat until you feel calm and present.

This exercise is not just useful in public speaking. You can use it any time you feel distracted in everyday life, perhaps before a stressful meeting or when you're about to yell at your children.

Breathe. And be conscious that you are breathing. It's simple. Remembering to do it is key. And practicing it on a regular basis makes it a habit.

## Presence

We will now take a detailed look at presence and what to do and *not* do to achieve the state of presence.

### The Presence "Formula"

In understanding presence, a big challenge is to satisfy the analytical part of the brain that strives to gain an intellectual grasp around the concept of presence. In actuality, presence is not a mental concept. We can talk about it, which makes it a mental concept, but in essence it's an experience.

When you experience presence, there is no sense of time. There's nothing but that moment. You feel completely connected to the energy of the audience. You forget your sense of *self*, which is the opposite of self-consciousness.

In practicing and teaching stage presence, I've found it useful for students to have visual steps or a structured practice to follow when practicing. That's what I'll share with you shortly. First, let me say that you can use the diagram below as a guide in conjunction with the structured practice. I've found the diagram to be especially useful for linear thinkers.

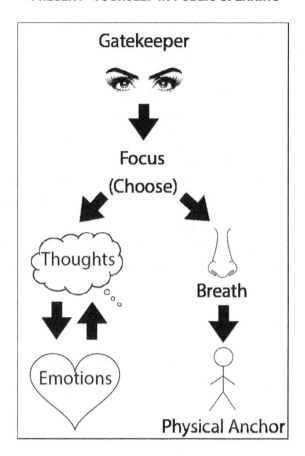

## Gatekeeper

The two eyes in the above diagram represent you, your consciousness, if you like, your awareness when you're looking out into the world. When public speaking, you're looking at your audience. You might think of your awareness as the witness, or the observer. I've even heard of it called the *third eye* in certain yoga and meditation practice. For the purpose of this conversation we're going to call your awareness the *gatekeeper*.

So you have eyes, you look out, and you see things. But there are different levels of seeing. There's seeing the detail, and there's zooming out, similar to a video camera. And then there's seeing internally what's happening in your own head. Have you ever noticed that when you're in thought you can get "lost" and become unaware of your surroundings? The moment you're aware of it, the gatekeeper part of you can say, "Oh, I'm in thought." And that's when you come out of it.

## Choose

Where is your attention right now? What are you choosing to focus on right now?

As the gatekeeper, you get to "choose" where your attention is focused. You can choose to think different thoughts. For example: *I'm choosing to shift my focus back to the current moment. I see the audience is sitting in front of me, I feel the temperature of the room*, etc. That's why in the diagram above, choosing comes before the thought bubble.

## Emotion

Thoughts lead to emotion(s).

Let's say you're thinking, "I'm so nervous. I'm not prepared for this presentation. I'm nervous." Your body chemistry is going to respond to that thought and create nervous energy, pumping more adrenalin into your body. Your shortness of breath is also a response to that thought, causing you to feel even more anxious. Your heart starts to pump faster. You might even start to shake from the adrenaline.

Your emotions are created by your body's reaction to a thought. That's what the arrows in the below diagram represent. The thought leads to the emotion.

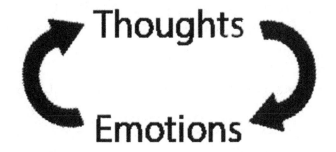

**The Vicious Loop of Thought and Emotion**

Continuing the above example, at this point, you feel even more nervous, which might lead to the thought, "Oh my gosh, I AM nervous. My heart is pounding out of my chest, and I can feel my face turning red." And that leads to your feeling even more anxious, which feeds the thought even more. It's like an endless loop, and you become stuck in it.

## Breaking Out of the Vicious Loop

So what do you do when you're stuck in this vicious loop of thought and emotion?

The first step is to notice that you're in the loop. That very act of noticing snaps you back to being the witness of your experiences, that *gatekeeper* part of you.

## Choosing a Different Thought

As the gatekeeper now, you can then CHOOSE a different thought. You can CHOOSE instead to focus on the physical anchor of your breath.

The gatekeeper in your head might sound something like this: *OK, calm down, I am aware that I am breathing, breathe slowly, breathe deeply into my belly. Breathe. I am aware of my breath. I'm in the moment. There's nothing else but this moment.*

## Physical Anchor—The Breath

The simple act of breathing and being conscious of your breath has a natural way of settling those swirling thoughts within your mind. As you saw earlier, it's like putting down the snow globe so that the snow flakes (thoughts) will naturally lose their momentum and the gatekeeper of your mind (the conscious you) will be able to see much more clearly. A pervasive calm is naturally created as a result.

So the breath and consciously choosing to be aware of your breathing is a powerful physical anchor. For example, when you are practicing this on stage, the dialogue in your mind might sound something like this:

*OK, I'm aware of my breath, I'm aware of my breath. Oh, that lady in the back is looking at me funny, I must be boring. Oh, I'm back in thought now. I'm back in the emotion of feeling anxious. OK, let that go. I'm aware of my breath. I'm breathing in. I'm breathing out. I'm breathing in. I'm breathing out.*

Every single moment, you have the choice. You always have the choice to consciously breathe and come back to presence.

## There's Only Ever Now

We tend to think of events in terms of past, present, and future. But really, there's only ever now. I'm going to prove it you. Are you ready? Raise your hand yesterday. Raise your hand tomorrow. Can you do it? Of course not.

My students laugh when I ask them to do this because they immediately get my point. The point being, you can only physically exist right now. And that's what conscious breathing does for you. It anchors you back to right now.

There's only ever now. There is no tomorrow really. It's always ever now. "Tomorrow" and "yesterday" are concepts that we hold in our thoughts. They don't exist in physical reality.

If you can wrap your head around that and embrace the fact that there's only ever now, there's no reason to be nervous. There's no reason to think all these thoughts and emotions because it's a little bit of a trap. The good news is that as soon as you notice it, boom! You're out again. You're back to being the witness, the gatekeeper.

## Presence Exercises

We've discussed presence in detail. By noticing

when we're in thought and emotion using our gatekeeper, our witness, we notice our breathing. We deliberately slow down our breathing to take us out of survival mode. We use conscious breath (I am breathing, and I am aware that I'm breathing) to physically anchor ourselves back to presence.

So what's missing? There's only one step left—the *experience* of presence. That's where the structured practice comes in. I'm going to share two such practices, one to do individually and another to do as a group.

## Presence–Individual Practice

You can practice presence by yourself. At any moment you can "cause" yourself to be aware of your breath by consciously "choosing" to be aware that you are breathing.

Here is the individual exercise for bringing yourself to presence:

*Start to notice your surroundings. What do you see? Don't focus on any one thing. You are not staring. You're being aware of your visual surroundings.*

## Body Scan

*Become aware of your physical body.*

*You're going to do a body scan, working your way from the bottom to the top.*

*You can do this with your eyes opened or closed.*

*First focus on your toes. You can even tighten or curl your toes if you wish. Now become aware of your ankles. Now become aware of your entire foot, one foot at a time. Do you feel any sensations in your feet? Tingly sensations? Pulsing energy? Heat?*

*Now move up to your knees. Become aware of your knees. Do you feel any sensations?*

*Now move up to your thighs. Become aware of your thighs. Do you feel any sensations?*

*Now move up to your buttocks. Become aware of your buttocks. Do you feel any sensations?*

*Now move up to your belly. Become aware of your belly. Do you feel any sensations?*

*Now move up to your chest. Become aware of your chest. Do you feel any sensations?*

*Now move up to your shoulders. Become aware of your shoulders. Do you feel any sensations?*

*Now move up to your fingers. Become aware of your fingers. Do you feel any sensations?*

*Now move up to your hands. Become aware of your hands. Do you feel any sensations?*

*Now move up to your wrists. Become aware of your wrists. Do you feel any sensations?*

*Now move up to your neck. Become aware of your neck. Do you feel any sensations?*

*Now move up to your face. Become aware of your face. Do you feel any sensations?*

*Now move up to your mouth. Become aware of your mouth. Do you feel any sensations?*

*Now move up to your nose. Become aware of your nose. Do you feel any sensations?*

*Now move up to your eyes. Become aware of your eyes. Do you feel any sensations?*

*Now move up to your ears. Become aware of your ears. Do you feel any sensations?*

*Now move up to your head. Become aware of your head. Do you feel any sensations?*

*Do a scan of your entire body. Focus on the internal sensations. Do you feel any sensations?*

## Emotion in the Body

*Do you feel any emotion?*

*If so, in what parts of the body are you feeling it? And what does it feel like? For example, if you're feeling anger, you might feel a tightness in your chest area. Perhaps some heat. If you are feeling sadness, you might feel a dropping sensation around your chest and heart areas.*

*Come back to being aware of your breath.*

*If you had your eyes closed, open your eyes.*

*Take a few deep, slow breaths, in and out.*

You can do this exercise or a shortened version of this exercise at any time, especially if you are feeling an intense emotion, such as when you are upset or feeling extremely anxious before a speech. You can do a body scan of yourself and find the emotion in your body even as you are speaking on stage. This will help anchor you back to the physical, a bridge to the present moment.

## Debrief on Practicing Presence—Individual Exercise

What insights came up for you during or after the exercise above? There is no right or wrong here. Write down the insights. You can use *Worksheet #7: Presence Exercise—Individual Exercise Debrief* in your companion journal.

### Presence—Group Practice

During my stage presence class, I have students participate in a group presence exercise. The consistent feedback that I receive is that it is a very powerful exercise of experiencing presence.

I have one person come up in front of the group, one at a time, to do this exercise. So if it is your turn to be in front of the group, I time you for one minute. For that one minute, there is no talking. What you're going to do is be present with each person in the group for 10 seconds each. How it works is that you look at person A for 10 seconds and get present with them. At the end of the 10 seconds, I ring my presence bell (literally), and you move on to look at person B for 10 seconds. At the end of the 10 seconds, I ring my presence bell again, and now you move on to look at person C for 10 seconds, etc., until your one minute is up.

Without fail, as I'm explaining this presence exercise to my class, the reaction is "We're going to do what?" and then giggles and laughter are heard. Why do you think that is?

The little voices in their heads are telling them this is going to feel awkward and weird. For many people it *will* be awkward. And that is part of the experience—to be present with someone and be present to those little voices running in your head while you do so.

Presence is just paying attention to the person, giving them your undivided attention. Remember the word *present* also means *gift*? And that's exactly what you're giving the recipient of your presence—the gift of your attention. In fact when you say you're giving a "presentation," the word "present" is built into the word *present*ing—or *gift*ing.

## Debrief on Practicing Presence—Group Exercise

After the group exercise of practicing presence, I ask participants to articulate the insights and feelings that came up for them about presence. There is no right or wrong response. Your experience is your experience, and it is valid. Here are some examples of responses from my participants:

- *We have a very hard time being present for others.*
- *I felt uncomfortable.*
- *It felt weird because there wasn't something I was trying to communicate in words. It was just space.*
- *I experienced a sweet spot, and there was nothing, no agenda. No hidden agenda. I was just paying attention. I felt peaceful.*

## How Do Insights about Presence Apply to Public Speaking?

When I ask my participants how their insights on and experience of presence can now be applied to their public speaking, the responses below are the most common with my commentary following each:

- **You don't need to be saying something to be present for your audience.**

A common behavior that I've observed of many people who speak in public is if they're given five minutes, they're going to talk for the **whole** five minutes without pausing. Part of why they don't pause is because they're not present. Pausing might cause their inner dialogue, their little voice to say, "Oh, that feels weird. This feels uncomfortable."

- *Being present can feel peaceful.*

If you're present during a presentation, you're anchored to the physical and not swirling around in your thoughts and emotions. That is peaceful.

- *Eye contact with the audience is important to convey presence.*

Eye contact and the quality of eye contact is very important to convey presence. Allow your audience members to look at you and allow yourself to look at them generously. You're not making eye contact for the sake of eye contact, even though it looks like the same thing. i.e., isn't eye contact just eye contact? The question to ask yourself is: are you actually seeing the person you are looking at?

For example, if I'm looking at the gentleman in the back wearing the yellow striped shirt, in my mind I'm saying, "Hello, how are you?"

- *Presence is honoring your audience members as individuals.*

When you're on the platform speaking, do you honor your audience members as individual people? Or are you in thought? When you're in the thought bubble as in the above diagram, you're not present with any one person in your audience in that moment.

## Mindfulness and Meditation

### *What Is Mindfulness?*

My favorite explanation of what mindfulness is comes from Jon Kabat-Zinn, author of *Wherever You Go, There You Are*, who said, "Mindfulness is paying attention on purpose, non-judgmentally, in the present moment as if your life depended on it." In other words, mindfulness is choosing to focus on focusing. It's attending to your attention.

---

## MINDFULNESS IS ATTENDING TO YOUR ATTENTION.

### —DR. AMISHI JHA, NEUROSCIENTIST, UNIVERSITY OF MIAMI

---

### *What Is Meditation?*

A great way to practice presence—and mindfulness—on a regular basis is through meditation. Meditation is a tool, an exercise if you will, a practice that trains you on your attention. When your mind wanders, you notice and you consciously bring your attention back to what you want to be focused on. There are many types of meditation. The one I find most useful is to focus on my breath.

## Neuroplasticity of the Brain through Meditation

I attended the inaugural Mindfulness in Business conference in New York City. There, neuroscientist Dr. Amishi Jha of the University of Miami presented her research findings on brain changes that take place in people who meditate on a regular basis over an extended period of time. In Dr. Jha's talk, she said that neuroplasticity is the brain's ability to re-organize itself by forming new neural connections throughout life. This is revolutionary because it was once thought that the brain was static. So we now know that the brain remains changeable even into adulthood. This is great news because it means we can train our brain for our benefit.

Dr. Jha also educated us on "intrinsic functional connectivity," which is the functional brain networks that work together. By observing blood flow in brain activity we see that it's different when our brain is at rest (calm) versus when we're focused on different things.

From Dr. Jha's research presentation, I learned that our brain is organized into three "networks" that are mutually exclusive. What this means is that the brain is only operating under one network at any given moment, not two or three simultaneously. The three networks are:

- **The central executive network**—this is the brain system that gets activated when a person is focusing. When you are *focused* on something, it is the central executive network in your brain that is being engaged.
- **The salient network**—this is the brain system that gets activated when you are *noticing* things.
- **The default mode network**—this is the default mode that your brain falls into. When you're neither focused nor noticing. Dr. Jha specifically points out that this is what many people refer to as "the wandering monkey mind" or that "internal chatter."

By practicing mindfulness on a regular basis through the tool of meditation and focusing (central executive network) on your breath, you are training your mind to notice (salient network) when you fall back to the internal chatter (default mode network), thus you teach yourself to more readily get out of that internal chatter.

## What Does All This Mean and What Are the Benefits for Public Speaking?

The message is this—meditating on a regular basis makes you less reactive and increases your mindfulness. You will be present more of the time, as opposed to staying in the default mode of internal thoughts, like a cat chasing its own tail. And when you're not present (and in that default mode network), you will be able to catch yourself faster and return yourself to the state of presence much more quickly.

When you're on the platform speaking and your mind starts to wander to thoughts of freaking out or giving in to the disempowering messages from your internal critic, the "muscle" that you've developed through the practice of meditation in noticing and re-focusing your attention back to the audience will kick in faster.

### A Simple Meditation Practice

Block off some time on your schedule. It can be as little as 5 minutes. Go to a quiet location where you won't be interrupted. Time yourself using a device with a gentle alarm. I personally use a free app on my smart phone called "Insight Timer."

You may close your eyes or keep them open. Take slow, deep breaths through your belly (not shallow chest breaths). You can put your hands on your belly to feel it rise in and out.

During this time, you don't need to "do" anything. All you are practicing is being the conscious witness—or gatekeeper—to your breath. You might even say in your mind, "I am inhaling. I am exhaling. I am inhaling. I am exhaling." Any time you notice your mind wandering off to follow a thought, gently bring it back to being aware of your breath. That's it. It's simple.

I recommend doing this simple meditation practice first thing in the morning before you get interrupted by the day's events. However, you can choose any time that works for you. The reason for doing it the same time each day is to build a habit out of it so you can adhere to it as much as possible. Remember, it can be as little as 5 minutes to begin with and then build it up over time, say to 20 minutes.

A quick note about some meditation technology that is so awesome that I must tell you about it! I also use a meditation technology device called Muse that helps me in my meditation practice. You don't need one in order to meditate, but I find that it has been very useful. In short, Muse is a brain sensing headband you wear on your forehead that fits over your ears similar to the way you would wear eyeglasses. It's connected to your smart phone/tablet via a free app that comes with the Muse head device. You choose a soundscape, e.g., beach waves. As you meditate (wearing the device), the sound of the beach waves get louder and louder when your mind is distracted. And the sound of the waves become calm and you hear birds chirping when your mind is calm.

To be honest, I was a bit skeptical at first, but now after six months of using it, I'm a convert. If nothing else, I think that the data it collects on your meditation practices over time is in itself an incentive to adhere to the meditation habit. You can learn more about the device at http://www.choosemuse.com.

At the time of this writing a Muse device is US$249. That can seem pricey, so I want to re-emphasize that it's definitely not a requirement in order to meditate. However, it is a great investment in my opinion.

And let me be clear—I'm not affiliated with this product or business in any promotional capacity—meaning I don't get any kickbacks for suggesting it to you. I'm mentioning it simply because I personally find it so valuable in my meditation practice!

# Beyond Survival Mode

When you can be present with your audience, you are no longer trying to survive your time in front of them. Rather, presence allows you to THRIVE in your message to the audience. You are operating in a very different mode.

I urge you to practice being present, both on your own as well as in front of an audience. Your experience of speaking on stage will be transformed, and you will never think of public speaking in the same way again.

# CHAPTER 5 GOLDEN NUGGETS

Being in the present benefits you greatly in public speaking because it takes you out of the "mind frick" and back into the present moment of being with your audience. Another way of looking at it is that presence is the quality of the attention you bring to your audience and an honoring of them with the gift of that attention.

Presence is being in the now. What distracts you from being in the now?

- Thoughts, emotions, and physical

How can you get out of that loop of swirling thoughts and emotions?

- You can use your *gatekeeper* to notice. Next you choose to use the breath as your physical anchor: *I am breathing and I am aware that I am taking an in-breath. I am aware that I am taking an out-breath.*
- Slowing down your breathing takes you out of the default internal chatter to anchor you back to the present moment. You cannot have stage presence without being present in the moment.

What can you do to practice being in the now and experiencing presence?

- Meditation is a tool of practicing focusing on your attention, and I highly recommend it.

Make it a priority and a daily practice to train yourself to be in the present moment, so when you are public speaking, you can escape the loop of thought and mind chatter (because you have trained yourself to do so), and "present" your message to your audience from a clear space. In this way, you won't simply survive your talk—you'll thrive and your audience will thrive with you.

# PART III

## THE PROCESS

MOST PEOPLE OVERESTIMATE WHAT THEY CAN
DO IN ONE YEAR AND UNDERESTIMATE WHAT THEY
CAN DO IN A DECADE.

—TONY ROBBINS

# CHAPTER 6

# THE PROCESS OF MASTERY

*We tend to minimize the things we can do, the goals we can accomplish. And for some equally strange reason, we think other people can accomplish things that we cannot. I want you to understand that that's not true. You have deep reservoirs of talent and ability in you.*

—Earl Nightingale

In this chapter, I shine a light on the process that is required to become a better public speaker—without sugarcoating it for you.

To be a fabulous public speaker, it takes much more than reading a book although that's a good start. You must have a desire to change and a growth mindset. You need to recognize habits and behaviors that prevent you from taking the necessary actions that will develop you into the public speaker you want to be, one who is confident, effective, and impactful to audiences.

Public speaking is a skill. I repeat—public speaking is a skill, and it can be developed. But for some reason, there's a misconception that you're either one of the "lucky" ones who was born with the public speaking ability or you're one of the "unlucky" ones, born without it. That is not at all the case. Just like someone who can't play the piano can learn and train to play the piano, and like someone who's never driven a car before can learn to drive a car—public speaking is a skill that you learn.

We're going to look at what it takes to acquire the skill of public speaking in detail. I will present a clear picture of what the path of mastering public speaking looks like and the steps to take to become a better speaker. You'll see that this path is continuous and is a life-long journey. The key is to continue even when things get difficult. You will receive useful suggestions on how to stay motivated as you walk the path.

In this chapter, we'll also look at the difference between a fixed mindset and a growth mindset, concepts we touched on in chapter 3, and how important it is to shift yourself to a growth mindset. I'll help you get crystal clear on your desire to change and help identify some strong reasons for you to do so. We look at the neuroscience of learning to understand how to train our minds to literally "grow memories." We also look at the importance of making public speaking a habit, investing in yourself and having a support team behind you to boost you as you go through the process of becoming a better speaker.

If you are sincerely ready to become a better public speaker, then I can tell you it takes a serious commitment on your part, a genuine desire to improve, and an investment of your time and effort. Unfortunately, many people have no concept of the amount of effort, dedication, and discipline it takes to develop a skill and the mindset required to continually refine and improve the skill further than *just OK*.

Many people are put off by this truth, and that's why my goal is to give you a process that you can follow to be sure you're moving forward in your progress. When you're learning a new skill or trying to get to the next level, it can be daunting when you hit a "plateau." Having a process you can trust and continue to follow is the key to getting "unstuck."

Get ready to immerse yourself fully in what it takes to develop your public speaking ability, gain clarity of what it takes to put yourself on the path in the first place, and learn how to keep yourself on it. If you trust in the process and in your own work ethic, the amazing speaker in you will emerge. You will be the witness to your own growth.

## Before You Begin

### EVERY MASTER WAS ONCE A DISASTER.

—T. HARV EKER

### YOU DON'T HAVE TO BE GREAT TO START, BUT YOU DO HAVE TO START TO BE GREAT.

—ZIG ZIGLAR

In the dojo where I train in karate, there's a big picture hanging on the wall with words that I love to read: *We do not seek to imitate the masters, rather we seek what they sought.* And what did the masters seek? They sought to walk the path of mastery. In this chapter we will look at the steps and elements that constitute the path of public speaking mastery.

As we begin, I'd like to highlight that in the world we live in today, there's so much emphasis on instant gratification and immediate rewards, so much so that many do not stop to appreciate that to build a skill from the ground up to a level of proficiency and beyond takes commitment, time, earnest effort, persistence, and discipline.

The *path of mastery* is not a linear one. In my experience, it looks more like an infinity symbol, and there is no "destination." There's always another level to get to. And that's where commitment, time, earnest effort, persistence, and discipline come into play.

I realize that not everyone who wants to learn to swim seeks to be an Olympic gold medal winner and not everyone who wants to learn to be a better public speaker seeks to be a professional, a trainer, or a speech contest winner.

My goal is not to push or convince you to win awards for public speaking. My goal is to bust the misconception that becoming a proficient public speaker is an overnight thing—or something a person is born with. It is not. It takes a growth mindset, dedicated practice, a hunger to improve yourself, as well as the desire to have an actual impact on your audience. After all, aren't we there to impact the audience with what we want to say?

It's not just about *surviving* the speech or presentation because our boss made us do it. Even if that is the case for you right now, I want you to look beyond that. Understand that once you're able to "survive" a presentation, it can open up new doors.

Being able to communicate with anyone, whether it's one-on-one or to a group, and to be authentic, sincere, and able to deliver your point powerfully leaves an impact. You can be an agent of change and transform people's lives through your words. Isn't that worth striving for?

I don't know where you're at right now, but I can tell you that by putting yourself on the path of mastery in communications can only help you. If nothing else, it will increase your confidence in yourself. And that is a wonderful thing.

### Desire to Change

I'm now going to be very direct with you—IF YOU DON'T PUT IN THE WORK, YOU WILL FOREVER REMAIN AT THE LEVEL OF A SPEAKER YOU ARE CURRENTLY AT. This is not me being mean—this is the highly likely probability.

Up until now, you probably didn't have a well laid-out process to follow. And that's what this chapter gives you. We dissect the process of mastery, so you will have a concrete understanding of what the process of improvement looks like, so you can then do the work to follow that process of improvement.

I'm going to be direct with you again—the process I'm about to show you will only work if you have a desire to change. No one can *make* you do anything. The drive to want to become a better public speaker, or even the best public speaker you can be, must come from within you.

You don't just wake up 10 years from now, and the skill has been bestowed upon you. It doesn't work like that. The hunger to be better has to come from within yourself. The more you desire to become a better speaker, the better your endurance will be to stick with the process and walk the path of mastery even when it feels hard.

Human beings are very much driven by the dichotomy of pleasure and pain. For example, notice these pleasure-based motivations about public speaking:

- *Public speaking gives me a thrill.*
- *I enjoy improving and becoming the best I can be. It lights me up.*
- *It fulfills me to communicate to a group of people.*

And here are pain-based motivations:

- *I'm so sick of being self-conscious when I speak in public.*
- *I don't want to have to be nervous and anxious anymore when I speak in public. I hate that.*
- *I no longer want to feel bad about myself when I speak in public.*

What's your motivation? If you're not clear, I'll be talking about the importance of having a strong reason later. Right now, the key attitudes I want you to take away from this section of the chapter are:

- Baby steps
  —And—
- Forward momentum

By focusing on the long-term goal of improvement and walking the path of mastery—through thick and thin—the "pain" of one speech won't derail you and cause you to exit the path of mastery. Here's a great insight from Tony Robbins on this subject:

*The real purpose of a goal is what it makes of you as a human being while you pursue it. Who you become as a person is the reward.*

By the time you're well into the process that I'm about to show you, you will have become a different, more empowered person. I followed this same process, and when I look back 10 to 15 years, I can definitively say that I have become a completely different person. Let me add that I am still following this process now, and I can tell you—I'm excited to meet the Mary of 10 or 15 years from now because I expect to look back to who I am today and not recognize myself once more.

I know you want to become the best version of yourself too, as a speaker and in life. That's why you're reading this book. Get in your seat of desire-for-change. Strap on your seat belt of hunger, and let's go for a ride on the path of mastery.

### Fixed vs. Growth Mindsets

Let's return to this concept that I first mentioned in chapter 3: fixed vs. growth mindsets. In *Mindset: The New Psychology of Success*, psychologist, Dr. Carol Dweck discusses her research results of people who have a *fixed mindset* versus those with a *growth mindset* and how a person's ability to learn and grow depends on which mindset they have, fixed or growth.

Dr. Dweck's research revealed that when it comes to a skill, the people with a fixed mindset believe that they either have the ability or they don't. They believe that they (and anyone, really) are either good at something or they're not. It's very black and white. This is a very limiting mindset because it puts a ceiling on a person's ability to learn and grow. They're also prone to avoid failure because to them, failure defines them. For example, if they failed an important math exam, they didn't just fail the test—they consider themselves a failure.

On the other hand, Dr. Dweck's research found that people with a growth mindset believe that if they put in the work and effort, they can improve a skill. The mindset here is *I can learn and get better at the skill*. To use the same example, if they failed an important math exam, it still hurts, but they respond by deciding, *I want to find out where I went wrong. Then I'll put in the effort, work harder, and get a better score next time. Let me learn from those people who got a better score.*

Dr. Dweck says that the key difference is that those with a fixed mindset say, "I'm not good at skill x," while the people with a growth mindset say, "I'm not good at skill x *yet*." *Yet* is the keyword.

Here is the good news—Dr. Dweck's research also shows that a person can shift mindsets. If you're aware that you have a fixed mindset, you can begin to shift into a growth mindset. Dr. Dweck, herself, admits that she used to have a fixed mindset and now has clearly adopted the growth mindset in her life for the better.

Dr. Dweck explains, "The growth mindset allows people to value what they're doing regardless of the outcome." She goes on to share, "Having a growth mindset doesn't force you to pursue something. It just tells you that you can develop your skills. It's still up to you whether you want to."

In order to become a better public speaker and to begin that development process to become the best speaker you can be, you need to adopt a growth mindset. Regardless of your past experiences with public speaking, if you work at it, you can improve. Train yourself to value improvement. The content of this book can help guide you to do just that.

## The Neuroscience of Learning

Dr. Britt Andreatta, the director of training and development at the online training company Lynda.com, in her The Neuroscience of Learning lecture explains that the neuroscience of learning is how the central nervous system and peripheral nervous system work together to create and retain new knowledge and skills.

Remember that special part of the brain called the amygdala that we talked about in chapter 2? It turns out that the amygdala together with the hippocampus, another part of the brain, play a major role in how humans learn. It's no surprise based on what we've already talked about. Let me explain what I mean.

The hippocampus unites the left and right hemispheres of our brain and acts as our "data drive," like a recording device that takes in learning, holds information, and pushes it out to the rest of the brain.

As we've already discussed, the amygdala is responsible for our flight-flight-freeze response. It takes in stimuli from our senses to assess if we're in trouble. If it senses trouble, it kicks off this fight-or-flight response and announces to the hippocampus, "This is important! Hit record, so I don't die next time. Remember this!" All of our senses are directly tied to this amygdala-hippocampus structure.

Developmental molecular biologist, Dr. John Medina explains this amygdala-hippocampus relationship using a particular metaphor—and one that I shared briefly in chapter 2. In *Brain Rules* Dr. Medina describes the amygdala's command to the hippocampus to record a troubling moment like this:

> The amygdala is chock-full of the neurotransmitter dopamine, and it uses dopamine the way an office assistant uses Post-It notes. When the brain detects an emotionally charged event, the amygdala releases dopamine into the system. Because dopamine greatly aids memory and information processing, you could say the Post-It note reads "Remember this!"

In other words—remember this and never have that situation happen again. *Don't do THAT again!!!!!*

This is why if in the past you had a terrifying experience of public speaking, you still remember it like it was yesterday. Your amygdala responded to this frightening experience as a perceived threat and made sure that this experience was recorded in your long-term memory to protect and deter you from ever wanting to repeat that same "threatening" experience.

However—you can train your brain to override the meaning of that initial experience. How? By doing it again and again, speaking in public repeatedly, until the fear impulse has been over-written so that your brain (hence, you) no longer perceives it as a threat.

## How We Learn—We "Grow" Memories

In her The Neuroscience of Learning lecture, Dr. Andreatta also explained that when we learn something and then we retrieve what we've learned , we literally grow memories. She states:

> Each time we fire that neural pathway, and that little electrical charge happens, it gets stronger, and they actually have measured the microns of how thick this dendron (neural pathway) is. It actually gets thicker and thicker the more you use it. We grow memories, and the more you activate information the easier it becomes.

Dr. Andreatta explains that changing contexts also aids in the retrieval-learning process. So if you retrieve what you learned in a different physical environment, it cements that learning into you even more. Even if it is in the same physical room where your first learning took place, but on a different day, that's a whole new context. She notes, "Changing context and activating the thing that you learned makes it go stronger, faster."

If we apply this to the knowledge and skill of public speaking, we would be best served in our public speaking growth to speak in front of as many different groups of people as possible on a regular basis over an extended period of time.

## Creating Structures That Keep You on the Process

> ### MOTIVATION IS WHAT GETS YOU STARTED. HABIT IS WHAT KEEPS YOU GOING.
>
> —JIM ROHN

### Getting Past the Hump

> ### SUCCESS IS RESERVED FOR THOSE WHO GO ON ANYWAY.
>
> —JIM BRITT

When we're attempting to learn a new skill, or go to the next level of an existing skill, it's common to feel an internal inertia called resistance. Author Steven Pressfield calls this the "shadow." This shadow, this resistance is the equal and opposite reaction that tends to come up when you want to do something to grow, such as practicing public speaking, going to the gym, learning to swing dance, etc. We need to be mindful of this resistance when it surfaces and not allow it to stop us taking forward action.

In the following examples, you'll see how this phenomenon of internal resistance gets played out with any skill you're trying to build:

Before attending my very first Toastmasters public speaking club meeting, I felt the jitters of not knowing what to expect. The resistance came in the form of little voices, like "Skip this week, go next week instead" and "You've had a rough day, take a break, don't force yourself." Every subsequent meeting after the first one, I felt a little less jittery and more and more at ease.

Similarly, when I first decided to learn karate as an adult, I experienced a great amount of resistance in getting myself to my first class. That apprehension did not stop after the first class—as I've already mentioned. I heard those little voices uttering things, like "Don't go. It's not mandatory. You don't HAVE to do this. What if the big guys hurt you? What if you look like an idiot? You're tired, take a break, you deserve a break." I felt the inner resistance of dread. For the first two to three months, every time I got in the car to drive to the dojo, I had to push through that.

In some ways, it's like a disagreement between your inner parent and inner child. The resistance is the inner child, declaring, "I don't want to and you're not going to make me." You must listen to the more mature and experienced inner parent because it knows what's best for you. That means taming your inner child voice through habits until you get over that hump of resistance.

And this taming does not just happen one time and then all resistance is gone. It's not that easy. With each new level of learning, there's a new hump to experience. And you just need to push past it each time.

## Forward Momentum

Improving your public speaking and communications skills is a marathon, not a sprint. Just the thought of a marathon can be tiring—again, you've got to watch those little voices and "catch" them as they are happening, dynamically, in the moment. Be objective. Use the 3Rs Process from chapter 3 to uncover those limiting self-beliefs, question their legitimacy, and objectively free yourself from that imprisonment.

So long as you are making forward progress, no matter how insignificant it seems, you're moving in the right direction. The key is—you're not allowing those little voices of your inner critic and the limiting self-beliefs stop you from taking steps forward.

## Baby Steps Count

If the process seems daunting at first, don't be discouraged. If you break a large task, like learning a new skill, into baby steps, it doesn't seem as daunting. In fact, if the baby steps are so small that you know you can do them, it helps you push past the inertia of beginning, so you can build some momentum.

And it is for this reason that I highly recommend Toastmasters. Attending regular club meetings will help you develop a habit, and it's a consistent venue to practice your communications skills. There's also the social reward of meeting and interacting with other like-minded individuals who are there to improve their public speaking skills, as well as support you in yours.

I myself have been a member of Toastmasters for about 15 years. I've made many friends from all around the world through the organization. It really was the environment that helped me realize, in baby steps, that public speaking doesn't have to be this "scary thing," and, instead, it can be an enjoyable experience that can also benefit others you're speaking to.

## Making Public Speaking a Habit

If you make public speaking a habit, sooner or later, it will become second nature to you. It will no longer be an infrequent event that you "have" to do. It will feel "normal" to you. This is the power of making public speaking a part of your life in a routine way.

To quote Dr. Andreatta again, "If you do something 20 times, you've started to make the neural pathway. By the time you get to 40, you've hit a habit, and by the time you get to 66, they actually measure the neurons getting thicker on that pathway."

Do you remember when you first learned how to drive? Each time you got into your car, you had to go through a checklist in your head. *Do I have the seatbelt on? Is the rearview mirror adjusted? Are the side mirrors adjusted? Is my seat adjusted to the length of my legs? Check the mirrors, are there any cars coming? Turn the blinker on, etc.* And now after years of driving, those are things that you do without much thought.

That is the power of building habits, and it's the same with making the act of public speaking into a habit. When I wanted to become a public speaker, I was making a living as a computer programmer. I designed my next career step to be a software trainer because I knew software, but I wanted to be in a role where I was "forced" to speak in front of groups each and every day.

I'm not saying you need to change careers; just make it a conscious choice to make speaking up in groups more of a regular occurrence. Consider making it a point to say something at work meetings, maybe volunteer to run a meeting, or perhaps even go to a Toastmasters club and sign up for a role at each meeting, no matter how small.

How can you make public speaking a habit in your life?

## Building Habits and the Reward

Of course, it is easier to build a habit in the first place if you have a strong motivator. A positive motivator is more powerful than a threatening one. "I must do this presentation well or I'm going to get fired" is a threatening motivation, so it doesn't work as well. On the other hand, "I want to become better at speaking in public, so I can go for that future promotion" might be a better one.

For me, my motivation was that I developed a love for the impact that I saw public speaking could have on the audience, and I got a rush out of that. It made me feel good when I saw that what I said made a difference to people in my audience.

We'll talk more about having a strong reason as a motivator shortly.

## The Process

Have you ever been told that to become a better speaker, you need to "practice, practice, practice"? Although this is true, this advice is very general and very high-level. What is the breakdown of the PROCESS of practice? What LEADS to the COMMITMENT to the process in the first place? Why do two students begin at roughly the same skill level, and student A takes on the learning and improves in leaps and bounds while student B practices once during class and never again? What drives student A to take on the process, and what impedes student B from continuing the process? And, by the way, what IS the process anyway?

To answer these questions, we need to understand the process holistically. We must see a complete picture of the process of how to become a better public speaker. To do this, I deconstructed my own process of building my public speaking skills. The process, as it turns out, can be applied to any skill you want to develop.

## The Inside-Out Approach's Path to Mastery

The diagram below symbolizes the inside-out approach's path to mastery.

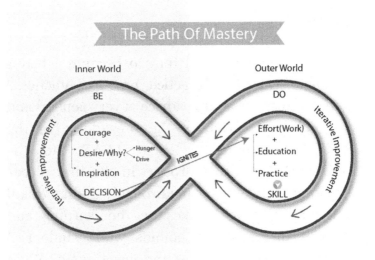

As you can see, the inside-out approach's path to mastery is not linear. Rather, it is an iterative path of improvement, represented by the infinity symbol. The path to mastery is infinite; there's no "destination." You can never "get there" or "reach the top" because whatever level you're at, there's always another level of refinement to the skill you're trying to improve.

It's no different with public speaking. There's nothing magical about the formula to becoming the best speaker you can be. You walk the path of mastery, do the work to keep on the path, and avoid temptation to exit the path. That's it.

In my public speaking workshops, I'll ask, "Does anyone here play a musical instrument?" There's usually at least one person who raises their hand. I'll ask, "How long did it take you to become competent at playing it?" The answers vary, but "At least 5 to 6 years" is a common answer.

Again, it's no different with the skill of public speaking. It takes time and effort to be a competent public speaker. You may not want to hear that because it sounds like such a long time, but it's true. If you are serious about becoming a better speaker, understand and follow the process of mastery described here. You'd be surprised at how much you can progress in even just one year.

## The Balance of "Being" and "Doing"—Yin and Yang

In looking at the diagram above, you may be familiar with some elements within it. I'll be connecting the dots and tying it all together for you.

If you draw a vertical line right down the middle of infinity symbol, the left side is the "inner world," or the *intangible* elements; and the right side represents the "outer world," or the *tangible* elements. This can be related to the nature of yin-yang. In Eastern culture, there's a well-known symbol called yin-yang.

Yin, the white parts of the circle, represent yin energy—feminine energy; and yang, the black parts of the circle, represents masculine energy.

Just as in nature where there is a balance between male and female, the masculine energy (yang) and feminine energy (yin), we have within ourselves both masculine driving-force energy (assertive, aggressive) and feminine receptive energy (nurturing, easy-going). The yin-yang represents both types of energy harmonizing in balance.

Just as yin and yang together produce harmony, the being and the doing together also produce harmony in the sense that it produces the result you are looking for, in this case, the skill you're trying to acquire. Without the "being" (yin) there would be no "doing" inspired. And without the "doing" (yang) there would be no "being" (yin) experienced.

## The "Be"

This is represented by the left side of the diagram. The "be" is what you bring to the learning process from within yourself. It is the driving force that comes from within you that propels you onto the path of mastery in the first place.

## The "Be"—Courage

To become a better public speaker, you need to get in touch with your own courage. You need to "be" courageous. We saw in chapter 4, the origin of the word "courage" comes from the French words "coeur" meaning "heart" and "age" meaning "time." So, *courage* really means: *a time for the heart*.

Why do you need to "be" courageous to improve in a skill?

- You need to "be" courageous to step outside of your comfort zone and act in spite of fear. It can be scary to do something you're not familiar with, that you're not good at yet.

Remember in chapter 2 we debunked the myth that those people with courage don't have fear? We discovered that courage only exists when there IS fear. Because without the presence of fear, there would be no need for courage.

- You need to "be" courageous to be willing to look at yourself objectively, without ego, to see what areas you need to improve in and to find the blind spots about yourself that may not be pleasant to look at.

- You need to "be" courageous to have trust in the process—even when it doesn't FEEL like you're improving. I assure you—you are IF you continue to follow the process.

- You need to "be" courageous to continue even when it feels like nothing is working.

- You need to "be" courageous to find help and ask for support when you feel stuck.

## The "Be"—Your Why

Why do you want to become a better public speaker? There is no right or wrong answer here. The point is to get crystal clear as to why you want to put yourself through the process to become a better public speaker. Your "why" determines your hunger and drive to become the best speaker you can be.

Your "why" can range from "I want to speak in public without passing out" to "I want to become a world-renown motivational speaker"—and everything in between.

The answer to your "why" is not as important as your being emotionally in touch with your own "why." Being (the "be") consciously present to your own "why" will naturally generate a hunger within you that drives (the "do") you to continue the process despite external. The stronger you're connected to your own "why," the higher priority becoming a better public speaker will be in your life. Excuses will fall to the wayside.

If you have a burning desire to improve, you will find a way to continue the process. As the motivational speaker and author Les Brown would say, "You've got to be HUUUUNGRY!!!"

You'll see in the section below "The Big "D"—Decision for Action—that it's your connection to the strong emotion of that inner drive and hunger that "ignites" the fuel in your "being" to inspire you to take the necessary "doings," meaning the actions to acquire the skill.

Your reason, your "why," will shift and change as you continue to improve. We'll discuss your reason in greater depth in the next section, "Desire to Be on the Path in the First Place."

### The "Be"—Inspiration

You won't go far in the process if you're not inspired to improve. Think of the word "inspiration" as being "in spirit."

At a coffee house, I serendipitously met an 82-year-old professional artist. He was sitting next to me drawing on his pad. I ended up having a three-hour conversation with him in which I learned so much about the creative process. The most important take-away from our conversation was:

---

## YOU MUST DO WHAT NURTURES YOUR SPIRIT.

---

What feeds your spirit? What brings you joy? Create time for these things on a regular basis. When you do the things that nurture your spirit and bring you joy, you're charging your own batteries. This, in turn, will give you the energy you need to continue your journey of becoming a better speaker. Let's face it, the process can sometimes be daunting and even painful.

For me, writing in my journals and free writing (writing without a purpose) bring me great joy and light up my spirit. So does connecting with friends who are on a similar wavelength. Philosophy, music, and poetry all feed my spirit. So does unabandoned fun, playing, dancing, singing, and martial arts.

Again I ask you—what feeds your spirit? Go do those things.

## The Big D—Decision for Action

Courage + a strong "why" + inspiration ==> Decision for ACTION.

When you have the courage and a strong "why" that you're clear about and emotionally connected to, combined with inspiration and that inner hunger, you have the fuel that ignites the decision for action. In essence, establishing a solid foundation of "being" propels you to "doing," which in turn adds greater solidity to your "being" such that you continue "doing," and the incredible back-and-forth continues as catalysts for one another . . .

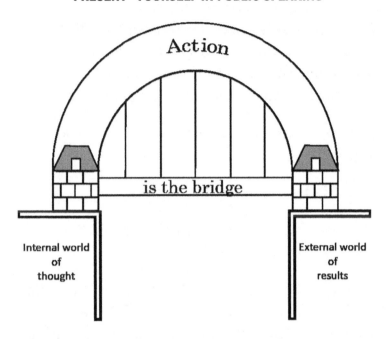

Action is the bridge

Internal world of thought

External world of results

You can feel all the courage in the world and know why you want to become a better speaker and feel inspired, but if you don't take action to create opportunities to speak in front of a group, it's all for naught. Your wishes will never materialize in the real world. What precedes the kick-off of an action into motion is a decision—a decision to take action.

In his book *Pivot: The Art and Science of Reinventing Your Career and Life*, Adam Markel distinguishes between two types of decisions, little decisions and big decisions, or big "Ds." You make decisions every day, like what you're going to eat for lunch, whether you'll drive route A or route B to get to work. These are the little decisions in your life. Big Ds are the decisions that affect you in bigger ways, like deciding to change careers or quit smoking—or DECIDING to FINALLY become a good speaker.

Here's the part that's most interesting. A big D is usually accompanied by intense emotions. For example, I experienced intense emotions right before making a big D to commit to learning karate. I was alone in my living room and thinking about my fears of physical confrontation. In a moment of clarity, I connected with the power within myself and saw the impact that this fear had on me and I saw how it has held me back. Tears poured down my face. If the tears could talk, they would have screamed, "Enough!" After that I committed fully to the process of becoming a martial artist. As of this writing, I've been learning karate for 18 months and am loving the process.

There are other authors who've reported having felt this emotionally intense moment that led to their big D decisions. For example, in Liz Gilbert's *Eat Pray Love*, she talks about that moment when she sat on the bathroom floor and just wept and wept. After which she makes the big D to leave her marriage and travel the world.

The late Dr. Susan Jeffers in *Feel the Fear and Do It Anyway* said she was so afraid of everything until one day she knew she'd had enough. She looked in the mirror, wept, and shouted at her reflection the words "Enough! Enough! Enough!" right before shifting her life from one of fear to becoming one of the most influential teachers of fear education.

The late Debbie Ford in *The Shadow Process*, said she had a moment also on her bathroom floor where she wept and knew she had had enough. After that she changed direction in her life from drug addiction to becoming one of the most powerful personal development teachers, helping people to fully accept themselves and their "shadows."

So why is there an intense emotion experienced immediately before a big D decision? What is the connection here?

The strong energy associated with the intense emotion IS the figurative *fuel* that IGNITES the decision for action (the figurative *fire*) to create the big change that you so desire in your life. Let's remember that a big change usually comes with multiple alterations in what has been your daily or weekly routine, many unknowns, and, therefore, big fears too.

Let's tie it all together now. You've reached a crucial point at which your intense desire for the change (fueled by the energetic output caused by the intense emotion felt when you finally surrender to your realization that ENOUGH is ENOUGH) has now EXCEEDED your fear of taking the action for change in the first place. So what's the result? You are ignited to take the necessary actions to manifest that change! You set the "doing" in motion—you create change!

In essence, the *formula* could look like this:

DESIRE for Change $>$ FEAR of Taking Action Ignites Taking of the Actions to Create the Change

## The Being "Ignites" the Doing

Your internal resources of courage, your "why," and your inspiration—all three integral components of your "being"— that lead to the big D to commit make up the fuel that *ignites* you to take the actions needed to acquire the skill—the "doing." Your internal "being" drives the "doing."

## The "Do"

This is represented by the right hand side of the diagram. The "do" is what you "do" in the learning process that is actionable. It is the tangible steps that make the bridge to producing results seen by the external world.

## The "Do"—Work (Effort)

To become a better speaker, you have to put in the effort. For instance, speaking in front of groups as many times as you can—whether it's a formal presentation or speaking up at a group meeting at work amongst your peers.

As I've said before, I highly recommend visiting a local Toastmasters club. This is how I got started in my practice. It's an international nonprofit organization where people who wish to improve their public speaking and leadership abilities come together to support each other through practice.

*Discipline*—to me, discipline means showing up even when you don't feel like it. And this is beautiful because you're building a muscle, a new habit out of true choice, until the new habit takes on a life of its own. But before that practice or activity becomes habit, you have to remember to make yourself show up. Your only job until then is to show up.

*Focused intention*—keeping a focused intention means reminding yourself of your intention to become a better speaker, or any skill for that matter, and then you allow that intention to be your "mission." I find it helps to write it down. Be HUNGRY for the skill and hold that intention clearly in your mind.

*Commitment + long hours*—it's commitment that drives the practice. And the practice takes time—hours, days, months, years, and even decades.

*Persistence*—what is persistence? It's the opposite of quitting. During the process of mastering a skill, you might feel frustrated at times when you feel like you're learning to walk all over again. You may walk away, but persistence pulls you back the very next day. Persistence is the action of someone who is determined. It's when you declare, "Whatever it takes—over, around, up, and through—I will make it happen."

## The "Do"—Education

To be the best you can be, whether it's being a public speaker or another skill, you need to gain the knowledge that you currently do not have. There are various means through which you can acquire this education: books, video learnings, attending seminars, workshops, conferences, or mentors.

Having mentors is a critical component of becoming a better speaker. It doesn't have to be a "formal" mentor. It could be learning from speakers who are further along the path of mastery than you are.

A common question my students ask is, "Where do I find mentors?" Mentors are all around. It could be a book you read that resonated with you and checking to see if the author offers trainings or coaching. It could be attending a professional association, like NSA (National Speakers Association) or ATD (American Talent Development), and connecting with people who are further along the path.

A key to synthesizing what you've learned is to reflect. We'll cover this in detail in the next section "Applying the Process to Public Speaking."

### The "Do"—Practice (Repetition)

If you want to become better at any skill, you need to practice. Public speaking is no different. Where do you practice? Anywhere you can. As I already mentioned multiple times, Toastmasters clubs are a great start. Toastmasters is the most consistent, safe, and supportive venue I know of to practice public speaking on a frequent basis. And regularity is a huge component of building a skill. Outside of Toastmasters, you can practice in your own community. For example, you can volunteer to lead a meeting at work or at your book club. You can volunteer to introduce a presenter. Any small amount of practice adds to the whole.

The key words here are consistency and regular practice. As I mentioned in chapter 2, you can use *Worksheet #1: Speaker's Log* in your companion workbook to keep a record of each time you practice. Each time you lead a meeting or give a presentation, even a practice presentation at Toastmasters, you record it in the log. This is tangible evidence that you're doing work in your practice, and it's a powerful visual reminder of your progress, which only adds to your incentive to continue practicing.

I want to repeat that practicing means showing up regardless of your mood. "I don't feel like it" is not a valid reason not to show up to practice. It's an excuse. It's the little voice of resistance. You can acknowledge you're having these thoughts and feelings, and still move your legs and get your butt to the practice floor. As Woody Allen once commented, "Showing up is 80% of life." Even if you have raw talent, that talent still needs to be honed and polished. That's done through consistent and regular practice.

## Doing the Work

---

# GENIUS IS 1% INSPIRATION AND 99% PERSPIRATION.

—THOMAS A. EDISON

---

## Mindset about the Work

My philosophy is never, ever stop being a student. The best mentors and teachers I've ever worked with are themselves excellent life-long students. I will not learn with anyone who has an *I-know-it-all* mindset.

---

# THE BEST MENTORS ARE THE BEST STUDENTS.

---

The mentors that I respect the most are those who have a "beginner's mind." No matter how many years of experience they have, they realize they can always learn more and there's always something that they can improve on. Those are the people I want to work with, whether they are my mentor or student. And that's what I want to impart to you: have a beginner's mind. You are always a student of learning.

## Do I Have to Do the Work?

Let's look at doing the work itself. You might be thinking "Ugh, do I have to do the work?" The short answer is YES.

Over a year ago at a conference, I had just given a keynote speech about this very topic. Afterwards, someone from the audience came up to me and remarked, "The work is the boring stuff. I want to hear the stories."

Yes, the work is not the most exciting step to hear about. But I'd be doing you a huge disservice if I didn't tell you that there is work. A lot of unglamorous, sometimes uncomfortable work is involved in becoming a better speaker.

Your mentality ought to be "short-term pain for long-term gain." The late master public speaker Jim Rohn said it best:

---

## YOU CAN'T HIRE SOMEONE TO DO YOUR PUSH-UPS FOR YOU.

---

Let that sink in. You can hire someone to *tell* you to do push-ups. You can hire someone to show you *how* to do the push-ups properly, but you cannot hire someone to do them *for* you. That's the work itself that's going to improve *your* muscles. Not his or hers.

This may sound obvious on an intellectual level, but you'd be surprised through my observations, how many people are not committed enough to find out what the work is and then do it.

Now that we have that covered, what *is* the work?

## What Is the Work?

The work is represented by the flowchart in the next section, "Applying the Process to Public Speaking." The steps you will see in the flowchart *are* the work. The work is an iterative process. The steps to the work include:

- Find out what your strengths are and incorporate them into your presentations.
- Find out the hard skills you need to develop. Then work on improving them.
- Find mentors who are ahead of you in the process.
- Listen to feedback from others, including your mentors, to see your blind spots. Then work on improving those areas.
- Be actively on the lookout to see what your limiting self-beliefs are. Then do the work of:

- Noticing them, acknowledging them, letting them go, and proceeding. You can use the 3Rs Process that we covered in chapter 3 to do this.
- The work is an iterative process. Continue the cycle again.

See how in the flowchart, the arrows point back to "Do the Work"? That's not a coincidence. Doing the work is at the end of every one of the steps.

And what is the work? The work is going through all the steps shown in the flowchart. See how it's pointing back to being self-reflective? That's because you do the work, you get some feedback, and then you reflect—*how else can I improve?* And then you do the work, and then you reflect—*how else can I improve?* It's an iterative and ongoing process.

## The Work Is an Emotional, Mental, and Physical Investment

I'd love to sugarcoat it for you and tell you the work is all roses and peaches, but I'd be doing you a great disservice because it's not. The work is not just an investment of your time; it's also an investment of your emotional and physical energy.

For example, when I was going through the World Championship, for my final speech, I spoke in front of 42 test audiences and collected written feedback sheets from people in my audience. I'd ask them, "What did you find confusing? What parts got you emotional?"

Below is a picture of the feedback sheets that I collected during those 10 weeks.

This is the pile of feedback sheets that I collected from my test audiences throughout my World Championship speech preparation process.

If I were to break it down even further, that work to speak in front of 42 audiences meant that I had to find and contact people to request a date and time to speak, put it in my schedule, drive to the group, give the speech, collect feedback, tweak my speech, reflect, rehearse the changes on my own time, drive to the next test audience (some were as far as 90 minutes away), practice, collect feedback sheets, and then it starts all over again. All of this was done outside of my full-time job.

For work-related presentations, the work isn't as involved—but let it be clear—there's still work. I prepare way ahead of time, do the necessary research, rehearse with co-workers, and get feedback—all before the "real" presentation.

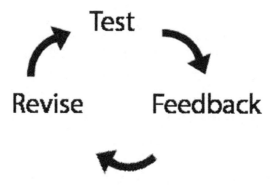

**The Work Is Work**

Let's face it, it's called "work" for a reason. It's not always fun.

There were times that I'd wake up in the morning and the *last* thing I'd want to do is go to another rehearsal. One group I rehearsed with met at 8:30 am . . .

Not everyone is willing to do the work, yet it's necessary if you want to have an impact with your message.

The thing to remember—what is on the other side of the work is so worth it. You will become a better and more confident speaker with a speech that actually impacts your listeners. And you will have grown in leaps and bounds as a person.

Seek out anyone who has ever accomplished anything, and you will find there was work, the grind that had to be done. Ask anyone who has lost a significant amount of weight, "Was it easy?" I guarantee they will say no. It takes work, discipline, and it's a process. The work is not always easy. It's tedious and sometimes painful.

So how do you "make" yourself do the work? That's what we'll look at in the section about reason and belief.

## Applying the Process to Public Speaking

I'm now going to break down how to specifically

apply the inside-out approach's path of mastery to your public speaking.

You can enter the inside-out approach's path of mastery at any point of skill level, whether you're a complete novice or already an expert.

The infinity symbol loops around again and again and again as you go from *being* to *doing* to *being* and back to *doing* again, all the while improving and refining your public speaking skill.

I'm now going to emphasize two components within the inside-out approach's path to mastery to show how they specifically apply to becoming a better public speaker:

Applying the Process of Mastery to Public Speaking

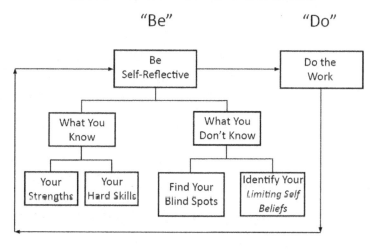

1. The courage to "BE" self-reflective (in the first loop of the infinity symbol).
2. "DO"ing the work (in the second loop of the infinity symbol).

## Breaking Down the Process into Essential Elements

A lot of people I train and coach are linear thinkers, analytical people, so it helps them if the process to become a better speaker is put into a process flowchart. For your benefit, you can follow the process flowchart above to ensure that you are on the path to becoming a better speaker.

- **"Be" Self-Reflective**

Let's look at being self-reflective. What does that mean?

To become a better speaker, have the courage to be self-reflective. That means looking at each of the following:

- *Strengths*

In chapter 3 we spoke at length about focusing on your strengths, incorporating your strengths into your presentations, and featuring them as main elements in your presentation. So (1) knowing your strengths is a part of being self-reflective, and then (2) you can do the work required to build on your existing strengths.

### • *Hard Skills (of the Craft)*

Being self-reflective also means looking at what hard skills you need to improve on and then doing the work. What hard skills in public speaking do you already know you need to work on? Perhaps, you use too many filler words, such as "um," "uh," "eh," "so," or "like."

Hard skills are related to the work you need to do for the content and delivery—the mechanics—of your presentation. Hard skills may include:

- Speech-writing skills
- Story-telling skills
- Vocal variety

### • *Blind Spots*

You also need to reflect on your blind spots. What do I mean by "blind spots"? Things you're not aware that you need to improve on. This is a little tricky. How do you know what you don't know?

### • *Listening for Your Blind Spots*

To determine your blind spots, you ask around. And then you listen. Listening is a very important skill. Speaking is only half of the communications equation. The other half is the listening.

Over ten years ago I enrolled in a six-month leadership course to improve my confidence. At that point I could speak and then sit down again, but I wasn't confident enough to get up in front of a room and announce, "OK, here's what we're going to do!" To me, that was what a leader was, and I didn't have the confidence to pull it off. This was an intensive course, with 50 participants and five coaches.

During a session, I had the opportunity to go up to the microphone in front of the room and share what I'd already learned about leadership from the course. At the end of the class, one of the coaches, Mrs. B. approached me and said, "Mary, what you shared up there was very inspiring."

I replied, "Thank you, Mrs. B. Tell me, what was inspiring about it?"

She answered, "Well, you were very stiff and very formal in your presentation."

I was confused. "Mrs. B, how is that inspiring?"

She explained, "Well, Mary, five years ago I was just like you, and you reminded me of how far I've come."

*Ouch!*

I listened—and what I discovered in this case was that I was too stiff and formal in my presentation. I just didn't realize because it was a blind spot. This was the self-reflection.

I enrolled in stand-up comedy and improv classes, and volunteered to do trainings at work to practice being more conversational on the platform. This was the work.

Here's another example—the year after my World Championship experience, a friend of mine introduced me to the late Dr. Ken Cranell, "legendary" professor emeritus of communication at Emerson College in Massachusetts from 1957 to 1999 (42 years). Dr Cranell had trained students in voice and articulation and authored a textbook of the same name, *Voice and Articulation.*

At his workshop I gave a prepared speech and was excited to hear his feedback. He asked, "Mary, are you aware that at certain points in your speech you go ultrasonic? That means your voice gets squeaky, and it's hard to understand you."

I responded, "Really? How squeaky?"

Dr. Cranell answered, "Only dogs can hear you!"

When I got home, I watched the video recording of my speech and, sure enough, at points when I was emoting excitement, my voice got high-pitched and was difficult to understand. This was the self-reflection. I worked on that. I focused on consciously lowering the register in my voice. This was the work.

What are *your* blind spots? Listen to feedback, reflect on it, and do the work to make corrections.

### • *Limiting Self-Beliefs*

Being self-reflective also means consciously looking at what limiting self-beliefs you have. In chapter 3 we spoke at length about limiting self-beliefs and how they compose the bottom layers underneath our disempowering "little voices."

To help you to identify and release your limiting self beliefs, you have the 3Rs Process. Doing the work is applying the 3Rs to your specific limiting self-beliefs, so you can liberate yourself from their hold on you. Beliefs, such as "I'm not qualified enough," "I'm not good enough," or "I'm not smart enough," will no longer stop you from continuing to take action to improve your public speaking skills.

- *Find Mentors*

I recommend finding mentors. Read their books, attend their workshops, as I did with Dr. Ken Cranell—and then reflect on what you learned from these sources. I'll talk about this in more detail in the upcoming section "Invest in Yourself."

## Applying the Process to Other Skills

You can use this process to learn any skill, not just public speaking. In fact, learning a new skill will likely reveal some limiting self-beliefs at points along the way.

## Learning a New Skill to Reveal Limiting Self-Beliefs

To help uncover your limiting self-beliefs, I recommend learning a skill that is finite and trackable, something you've always wanted to learn so that your motivation to do so is already there. Give yourself a finite amount of time to learn the new skill. At the end of this period, you'll be able to objectively determine, "Yes, I succeeded" or "No, I didn't succeed." For example, learn to play a song on the piano, learn how to swim, or learn to drive a stick shift vehicle.

As I shared already in chapter 2, a skill I had always wanted to learn was to solve the Rubik's Cube. I knew that applying the process of mastery to learn this skill would reveal my limiting self-beliefs, and I was ready to see them.

My husband served as my mentor, teaching me the skill of how to solve the Rubik's Cube. Often after he would give me instructions, I would admit, "You lost me." He'd restate the instruction in a different way, and I'd again say, "You lost me again." This would go on and finally I'd mutter, "Forget it. It's too hard." That's when I saw it—a limiting self-belief I had was "It's too hard."

Once I uncovered my limiting self-belief, I was determined not to have it stop me. I committed to spending one hour a day for up to 30 days. And every time the limiting self-belief, "It's too hard," came up, I noticed it, acknowledged it, and kept going, without buying into it. When it came up yet again, I persevered. I reminded myself that it was an illusion and continued.

At the end of 19 days, I was able to solve the Rubik's Cube. That evening when I finally put it all together,

I sat and solved it 16 times in a row, just to make sure it wasn't a fluke!

## Limiting Self-Beliefs and the Process of Mastery

There's a lesson here—don't allow your limiting self-beliefs to derail you from the learning process or the process of mastery.

Limiting self-beliefs don't have to stop you. And when you become aware of them and move forward anyway, you gain confidence and begin to see them for what they are: false beliefs from the past, not the "truth." You build a muscle of trusting yourself.

You can use the 3Rs Process in chapter 3 to work through your limiting self-beliefs. The better you understand your limiting self-beliefs, the less hold they have on you.

# Desire to Be on the Path in the First Place

### A Strong Reason

Remember that on the path of mastery, one of the key internal components is your "why" and how that "why" drives your hunger to become better. Now we're going to investigate your "why" to give you a better grasp of its importance.

## How Do You Make Yourself Do the Work?

You have to have a strong reason to want to improve. That's what helps drive the discipline. Otherwise, you will quit. Thus, the bigger your "why," the easier the "how."

Why do you want to become a better speaker? You don't have to. You can stay at the level you're at, and that's a choice. There's nothing wrong with that. But you bought this book and are investing time to read it, so I suspect you want to become a better speaker. Again I ask you—what is your reason? Don't just answer, "I want to be a better speaker" or even "I want to be a great speaker." That may be true, but I'd encourage you to look deeper.

Whatever the answer, I invite you to choose one that moves you. It ought to either inspire you or pain you so much that you leave yourself no other alternative but to succeed in becoming a better speaker. Check in with your heart to see if your "why" moves you. Here are some examples:

- *Do you want to set a good example for your children?*

- *Are you just so sick and tired of the anxiety that sucks up so much of your energy every time you have to speak in front of a group?*
- *Are you so sick of being afraid?*
- *Do you know there's something inside of you that you want to share with others that's going to make a difference in their lives?*

Take some time to get in touch with your "why(s)" about becoming a better public speaker. This is not just an intellectual exercise. You want to be very honest with yourself and allow yourself to *feel* the reason(s) that appeal not only to your head, but to your heart.

Again I ask you—what is your "why"? And does it move you?

Your reasons can change over time as well.

For me, my initial "why" of wanting to improve my public speaking was: I was just so sick of feeling self-conscious. I knew there was value deep inside of me that could inspire others if only I could get out of my own way and get over my own self-consciousness.

I also wanted to honor my late mother. My mum passed away from ALS in 1998. She was one of those people that did everything for her children. She moved to a country where she didn't speak the language. She worked many labor-intensive jobs. At one time, she had four part-time jobs at the same time. She worked many Saturdays and Sundays so that my siblings and I could have a better life than the one she had.

I want to reach my full potential so that I can uplift and transform lives with my words. I want to affect as many people's lives as possible for the better so that all of the suffering and sacrifices that my mum made for me weren't for naught.

Every time I say that, it moves me.

Today, I am still on the path of mastering public speaking. And I do mean "master" because mastery is not a destination, it's a path of continuous improvement and refinement.

You need to be crystal clear on what your reason is right now. The stronger you feel about your reason, the more intense your motivation will be to do the work required.

What is your reason for becoming a better public speaker? Spend a few moments now to reflect and write down your reasons. There is no right or wrong. When you find the reason that moves you, you'll know you're in alignment with your own truth. You can use *Worksheet #8: Have a Strong Reason.*

*What is Your Reason?* in your companion workbook to record your "why."

# Common Traps That Can Derail You from the Path of Mastery

### The Trap—Feeling Bad about Yourself and Your Progress

A common trap that can derail you is feeling bad about yourself and your progress because even after you make a few speeches and do a few practices, you may feel like your skill level and confidence aren't there yet.

Rather than focusing on how far you have to go, focus on the fact that you are making forward momentum. Skills need time to develop. A mentor once used an analogy I'll always remember. He said the following:

> When you plant bamboo and water it, after one year it looks like no growth has happened. In year two, still very little growth. In year three still nothing. At this point you might be wondering if you're wasting your time. But you continue to water and nurture this plant. In year four, still very little growth. But—and here's the cool part—in year five it grows to 90

feet in 30 days. So what was it doing in the first four years? The answer is, it was growing roots, a foundation, so that when it does grow tall, the roots can support its structure.

The Chinese Bamboo is one of the strongest plants on the planet. The bamboo is used to support the construction of high-rise buildings in many Asian countries.

Just as you are growing your public speaking roots each time you speak in front of a group of people, remember that your roots need time to grow. Just because you don't see immediate results, it doesn't mean you're not growing. Stick with the path of mastery, and your commitment and hard work will pay off. Be patient and don't be too hard on yourself.

## The Trap—Comparing Yourself to Others

Resist the temptation to compare yourself to others. Comparing yourself to others is a mark of the ego. The only detail you ought to be interested in is how much better of a public speaker you are now than one year ago. This is the only true mark of your progress.

## The Trap—Taking Feedback Personally

Here is a tip—DON'T. Whether you asked for the

feedback or it came unsolicited, don't take it personally. Some are well-intentioned and others may not be. If you receive negative feedback that doesn't resonate with you, you can use it as fuel to bring out the best in you.

During one presentation rehearsal, an older man in my audience stood up and shouted with his face red with emotional intensity, "What you said doesn't make sense, it's all wrong!!!" I could see the other members of the audience gasping as if to say, "I can't believe he just said that."

But I was calm because by this point, I'd seen it all. How could I get flustered? I was the one who was asking for feedback. When you're ASKING for feedback, you're going to get it. And feedback can come in all formats. It's all JUST feedback.

The more experience you have at getting and receiving feedback, the thicker your skin will grow. I'm not excusing people's behavior. Not everyone is kind and compassionate in their delivery of feedback. In my experience, some people come across as rude or even obnoxious. But it can happen. And when it does, know that it says more about them than it does you.

After I got home, I seriously considered what the man was referring to in his feedback, and I actually saw how his anger may have been triggered. I re-worded the presentation a little to avoid triggering anyone in an unpleasant way. I used negative feedback as fuel to improve my speech further—and so can you.

But to do that, you *must* avoid the trap of taking feedback personally.

## Help Along the Way

### Invest in Yourself

Going back to the path of mastery—remember the second component of the "doing" was education? Let's examine education more fully to give you a greater understanding of the spectrum of education available to help you develop your public speaking that much faster.

One of my favorite mentors taught me this:

### YOU CAN'T CHEAP YOUR WAY TO THE TOP.

—ED TATE

You must invest in your own growth. And it's not just money. It's also your time and effort.

## Read More Books

Make the time to read more nonfiction books to broaden your mind. I heard that many people do not read another nonfiction book after they graduate high school. That is sad because there are so many people who have points of view to share, wisdom, tools, and information that we can benefit from. But you need to be proactive and seek it out. I know you're not a person in that category because clearly you sought out this book. Congratulations!

I aim to read at least two nonfiction books per month, and I can tell you that if it weren't for other authors' valuable ideas and wisdom, I would not be where I am today. Some of my mentors even read one book per week.

Be hungry to continue learning with an open mind. Have a beginner's mind. No matter how much you think you know about a topic, you will continue to learn more if you are humble and have a beginner's mind. This is one of my favorite quotes about learning:

---

## THE MOST DANGEROUS WORDS IN THE ENGLISH LANGUAGE ARE "I KNOW THAT."

—T. HARV EKER

---

## Attend Personal Development Seminars

I can't emphasize enough the importance of attending personal development seminars. You will grow exponentially. Through the insights and experiential breakthroughs you can release limits that you didn't even realize you had or hadn't even been able to articulate.

You may not "think" that personal development seminars have anything to do with public speaking, but let me remind you that *you* are the common denominator. As we discussed in chapter 3, Empowering Yourself, the areas of your life are like a tapestry. All threads are connected.

I've personally attended Landmark Education courses, Peak Potentials courses (now called New Peaks), Omega courses, and many more. In 2007, I attended Tony Robbin's Unleash the Power Within seminar where I walked across 12 feet of hot coals. Learning to get into "state" to do what I needed to do is a skill that I don't take for granted. In 2008, when I attended Peak Potential's Enlightened Warrior Training Camp, I developed a muscle to break through my fears and limitations, which gave me direct access to the presence within myself that I now tap into when I'm public speaking.

You are capable of so much more than your current limits tell you. As one of my mentors along my journey explained, "People are sleeping giants. They are powerful beyond measure, but they just don't know it." This is what I want to awaken within you—your giant within. And a great way you can tap into that is through experiencing personal development seminars.

There are people I've spoken to who have preconceived judgments around personal development seminars. If you are one of these people, I'd like to ask you to pause for a moment and be mindful of what your little voice might be saying. I recommend you put that inner dialogue aside. I'm not asking you to believe me; I'm asking you to try it out and see for yourself. You can always come back to your original assertions if you choose to. Chances are, you won't want to.

What have you got to lose—except your limitations?

Have an open mind. Be willing to take action, engage in your life, learn from others, break through your fears and preconceived notions of yourself, and be ready to amaze yourself on the other side.

You can find some of my own recommendations of personal development seminars that I've attended and got a lot of value from.

## Attend Skills-Specific Workshops

When you want to target a specific skill within the craft of public speaking, you can find and attend workshops or education series that address that exact skill.

For example, in 2007, I became aware that I was too serious and stiff during my presentations. I needed to work on my humor skills. As mentioned earlier, I found a local stand-up comedy workshop series taught by professional comedian Bob Gautreau. In this ten-week series I learned humor techniques and got to write my own five-minute humor routine. I got feedback from the class and got coached by Bob. On week ten the class got to perform our humorous material in front of guests.

Attending this workshop series opened up the world of humor for me. I learned that humor is a skill you can learn and develop. I was so inspired by my experience that I signed up for Bob's advanced stand-up comedy series and his improv workshop series to work on my creativity on the platform.

What skill do you need to work on with which local workshops can help you?

## Seek Out Free Learning

There are so many trainings courses you can attend, even for free. Believe it or not, I find so many great talks, podcasts, and interviews that I learn from for free on YouTube, Sound Cloud, and iTunes. Just plug in the search terms you are looking for and—*viola*—they're available at your fingertips.

Google is also a great source of information. I find tons of useful articles for free.

## Attend Training Courses, Online and In-Person

There are many online courses you can take to expand yourself mentally. Lynda.com and Atomic Learning are two that come to mind. Some public libraries even have free subscriptions for people who hold library cards. For example, Boston Public Library.

If it's important enough to you, you will do whatever it takes to become better. Because the World Championship was so important to me, I attended many seminars, including listening to audio CDs as well as flying out to where the seminars were physically taking place.

To better understand the nuances of the mechanics of public speaking, I attended a large number of courses offered by Champions Edge led by Darren La Croix. I serendipitously won Doug Stevenson's Story Theater audio CD because I attended an NSA meeting (National Speakers Association), and they happened to have a free raffle that day. I remember I played that CD in my car over and over again, more than 50 times. I almost knew it by heart, to the point that I could recall his points and implement them live during presentations. Again, you can find a list of training course that I have personally attended and benefited from tremendously.

The point—I believe that anyone can become an amazing speaker. But not everyone wants to or is willing to put time and effort into doing that. A chunk of that time and effort will go to online and in-person training courses.

### Attend Toastmasters

All the learning in the world isn't going to help you to improve if you don't practice. For that reason, I highly recommend Toastmasters' International. I've already mentioned it multiple times throughout this book. It's a great place to practice with a safety net.

As already noted, Toastmasters is a nonprofit organization with over 250,000 members across the world. Toastmasters club members are supportive and also working on their own public speaking and leadership skills. Go to their website http://www.Toastmasters.org and click on "Find a Club" to find a local club that suits your availability.

I can tell you that I personally owe so much of my growth to attending this organization and then later leading within the organization. At the start of my journey, I used Toastmasters as an environment to practice not being self-conscious and to practice the mechanics of the craft of public speaking. When I became a professional speaker and trainer, I used the club meetings to practice new material and get feedback. My mentor Ed Tate also uses clubs to practice new material. He explains, "I would never practice new material in front of paying clients." I strongly agree.

## Learn from Mentors

I think it's obvious to people why mentors are important, but a common question I get asked is "Where do I find mentors?" I can tell you the way I've been the most successful in getting mentors is to show up to where they are, absorb what they teach, and put it into practice. By doing that you build credibility with them as a "serious" student and not just someone who's going to waste their time.

For example, one of my mentors, Darren LaCroix, has a "book test." When someone asks him to mentor them, he tells them to get a book he recommends. The next time they approach him, he asks, "Did you get the book?" If their answer is no, they're finished. They're not a serious student.

I've found that another good source of mentorship is to invest in yourself and take a training course that a potential mentor is offering. This way, the person gets to know you, and that investment can yield returns in the form of mentorship.

Going back to Ed Tate's words, "You can't cheap your way to the top," you can receive mentorship on a more formal basis where you invest in mentorship programs that your potential mentor may be offering. In short, go where they are and ask them specific, well thought-out questions.

### Hire a Coach

Don't underestimate the value of a professional coach who can help you move in the right direction. A coach can also be a great source of mental and emotional support. They can act as a sounding board and help to bring you back into a space of productivity when you're lost in self-doubt, freaking out, or even spiraling down to states of anxiety.

Professional athletes have coaches. There are life coaches, career coaches, and, yes, even speech coaches. To find a coach, you can do a Google search, but do your due diligence and be sure to check out their credibility.

## Return on Investment

When I look back over the past 15-plus years of my life on what I've done and achieved that was important to me, I can see a clear pattern—when I invest in myself through self-education, my progress is accelerated immensely. Investing in myself has saved me a lot of time and energy in reinventing the wheel to decipher the whats and hows. It's also helped me achieve many mental and emotional breakthroughs that have helped me get out of my own way.

## Your Support Team

Your support team consists of people who support you in your endeavors of becoming a better speaker, both directly and indirectly.

Let me describe to you my support team: when I am creating content, such as writing a speech or a book,

I have a regular baby-sitter who watches my two-year-old. The baby-sitter is a member of my support team. I have a good friend whom I share my vision and goals with. She is a part of my support team. I have an accountability buddy who is on a similar path to mine who's also using her business to help others realize their dreams. We hold each other accountable to take action on what we say we want. We also encourage, motivate, and support one another. She is most definitely a part of my support team. My mentors, people whom I meet at events whom I connect with, can share stories with, and bounce ideas off of, are all "members" of my personal support team. And, of course, my husband.

Who are the members of your support team? No one can achieve anything great on their own. It's easier to push a boulder up a hill with many hands helping instead of just your own, so don't underestimate the power of a support team. Invest time to build relationships with like-minded people and those who support you in everyday life too.

### Create a Network Map

Many years ago, I attended a leadership course during which I was introduced to the idea of a network map that features all an individual's various connections and relationships. It was a valuable exercise, and you can create one for yourself.

Get out a large piece of paper. Write "Me" in the middle. Then brainstorm all the areas of your life where you have connections with people, i.e., communities you belong to. For example, professional associations you're in, recreational communities you're involved with, work, businesses, interest groups, etc. Draw circles around each of these communities and spikes linking them. Paste this page on your wall. Share with people in your community what you're up to, and you'd be surprised how supportive people in various circles can be.

This is your go-to map to create connections with others and build mutually supportive relationships.

## Seek Positive Reflections

At an event I attended, an author/speaker spoke about having people in your life who reflect back positive versions of you. I love this concept. You need people around you who see your value even if you temporarily forget it. These are the people you want on your support team. On days or moments when you feel less than ideal about yourself, these are the people who can help straighten you out.

---

# YOU ARE THE AVERAGE OF THE FIVE PEOPLE YOU SPEND THE MOST TIME WITH.

—JIM ROHN

---

Jim Rohn's observation in the above quotation has been my experience. Get around people who are working on improving their public speaking skills.

## Stay Away from Negative People

As I mentioned earlier, in your endeavors to become a better public speaker and person, stay away from negative people. If members of your family or a co-worker is constantly spouting out negative comments or complaints, do your best to minimize contact with them. Energy is contagious.

# CHAPTER 6 GOLDEN NUGGETS

The goal of this chapter is to demystify the black box of how to become a better public speaker.

- To walk the inside-out approach's path of mastery in public speaking, you need to have a growth mindset. This is a mindset that believes a skill can be developed versus a fixed mindset that believes you're either good at something or you're not.

- Don't let limiting self-beliefs or other common traps, such as your ego and comparing yourself to others, derail you from the path. Instead, notice the limiting self-beliefs or ego traps, and continue to take action along the path in spite of them.

- You can enter the path from any skill level. Entering the path requires courage, a strong reason, and some inspiration.

- Muster the courage to be self-reflective. Be clear on your "why" and fuel your batteries with inspiration. Your "being" recruits the actions, the "doing," which is the bridge to manifesting your desired skill.

- Doing the work is being proactive in investing in your own continuous self-education and practice.

- Along the inside-out approach's path to mastery it's important to have a solid support team by your side, cheering you on and holding you accountable to your growth.
- The inside-out approach's path to mastery is iterative. There is no destination.

All these elements together compose the inside-out approach's path to mastery to becoming a better speaker.

# CHAPTER 7

# WORDS OF ENCOURAGEMENT FOR YOUR JOURNEY

We've now established that walking the path to becoming a better speaker is not an instant one and there will be points in the road where it might feel difficult. As a human being, you do face challenges that have the potential to derail you from your well-intended path. This is why this final chapter, Words of Encouragement for the Journey, is so necessary.

A wise mentor of mine, John, once said:

---

## DON'T LOOK AHEAD TO SEE HOW FAR YOU HAVE TO GO. RATHER, LOOK BEHIND YOU TO SEE HOW FAR YOU'VE COME.

---

And this is the essence of chapter 7—as we come near the end of the book, I want to send you on your way, full of motivation, zest, and eager anticipation to walk your path of becoming a better speaker—from the inside out.

Additionally, I want to warn you of the common potential potholes on the journey so that you'll be able to see them a mile away and steer in a different direction to miss them. And when you do hit those inevitable bumps in the road, I want to prepare your "suspension" of resilience so that you'll be able to zoom back out, pick yourself back up, and continue the journey of becoming a better speaker.

## Zoning Your Zones

### Understanding and Dissecting Your "Zones"

I love this depiction of zones. I first heard it described this way by leadership trainer and past World Champion Public Speaker, Otis Williams Jr.

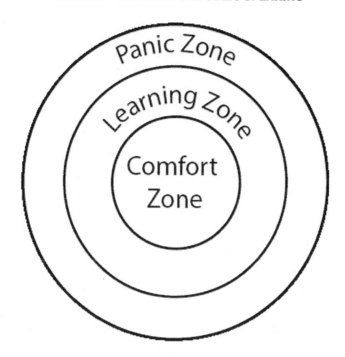

## Your Comfort Zone

The innermost circle is your comfort zone. This is what you're already familiar with, and you are quite comfortable performing tasks in this arena. For example, for public speaking, your comfort zone might be speaking to a group of four or less people on a topic that you're very familiar with for less than five minutes.

## Your Learning Zone

When you stretch a little outside of your comfort zone, you're in your learning zone. In this zone, you feel some discomfort, but you're aware this is where you learn new skills. It might be a little scary, but the discomfort is acceptable to you.

Getting up to speak in public for the very first time would have been—at one point—in your learning zone. When I first entered the professional speaking circuit, doing my very first paid gig was operating in my learning zone at the time. Other examples of being in your learning zone include if you're quite comfortable giving presentations and now you want to stretch beyond that to include interactive dialogue with your audience, the facilitation of games, or the incorporation of a Q and A (questions and answers) section in your talk. For some people it's speaking to a group of people that they find intimidating, such as a room full of presidents and vice presidents of a company.

You'll know when you're in the learning zone because it's whatever that next level is for you that makes you a little scared but perhaps also a little excited. You will learn and grow when you're in this zone; hence, the name.

### Your Panic Zone

This is going way beyond your comfort zone and even beyond your learning zone. Your panic zone is so far outside of what you find currently tolerable that it scares the heck out of you and sends you into panic mode.

## Taking Lessons from Swimming

In chapter 6 we talked a bit about taking baby steps. I'm now going to add to that the context of expanding your learning zone, little by little.

When I was seven years old, I took swimming lessons for the first time. I was a complete beginner. I didn't even know how to float on water, much less swim. Thank goodness my swimming teacher, Lydia, was empathetic. I remember that for weeks and weeks, she helped me work on just getting comfortable in the water. First we were in the little pool where I would wade through waist-high water. As I got more comfortable with the water, Lydia moved me up to the shallow end of the bigger kids pool. The water was still waist-high, so it wasn't too scary. And once I got comfortable with that, she moved me a little farther up in the pool to chest-height water; then after that, to neck-high water. With a foam kickboard, I learned how to float and then eventually to float without a kickboard.

Lydia was an excellent coach. She understood the power of the learning zone. By continually keeping me within my learning zone and stretching my learning zone out, a little at a time, I learned the skills that I needed without ever entering the panic zone.

Even when I eventually hit the deep end of the pool for the first time where my feet couldn't touch the ground, Lydia put a hula hoop around my chest attached to a rope that she held from the side of the pool. I felt a little scared but also knew she wouldn't let me go.

## The Inch-by-Inch Approach to Public Speaking

Why am I telling you about how I learned to swim and what has it got to do with public speaking?

Lydia's approach in coaching me how to swim is the same approach I use with my public speaking students and clients. It's the same approach that I recommend for you. By continually stretching the outer rim of your learning zone, a little at a time, you're consistently growing with mild discomfort as your companion—it's tolerable but not too scary. You don't need to enter your panic zone to learn. It's like when you want to build muscles, you go to the gym but don't lift 100-pound weights on the first day. You might lift 10 pounds for a couple of weeks, then move up to 15 pounds, then 20, etc., until you get to 100 pounds.

## The Deep-end Approach to Public Speaking

There are some teachers and coaches whose methodology is to throw you into the deep end—the panic zone. While, perhaps, there is merit to that in some instances, pushing someone so far outside their comfort zone beyond their learning zone and directly into their panic zone can be detrimental because what happens when panic sets in? The student goes into survival mode. They become scared to death, and their openness to further learning going forward may completely shut down.

For some people, this may help their learning after the fact when they're calm again and able to reflect. But I would say that is more the exception than the rule. Rather, I suspect many people's reaction would be to become so turned off by the experience of pain and panic that the tendency would be to avoid going back any time soon, possibly ever. That would sadly defeat the purpose of learning. This is why I recommend the inch-by-inch approach, always within your learning zone, so you don't end up giving up altogether on the learning and growth.

You may have had that panic experience with public speaking in the past, but you're reading this book, so I suspect you're ready to jump back in the figurative pool—this time trying the inch-by-inch method.

## Don't Stop before You Begin

A common trap when contemplating learning a skill, such as public speaking, is that people imagine themselves in the panic zone and get scared off *before* the learning even takes place. To become a better public speaker, your first presentation doesn't have to be in front of the president of your company, or the president of the country for that matter. It would help to begin in a supportive group environment, such as Toastmasters International, and work your way up from there.

"Zoning your zones" is about challenging yourself to improve, learn, and grow inch-by-inch—and more importantly—so you don't give up before you even begin.

## Never Ever Ever Ever Quit

In Winston Churchill's famous speech on October 29, 1941, at the Harrow school, his alma mater, he said:

---

### NEVER GIVE IN, NEVER GIVE IN, NEVER, NEVER, NEVER, NEVER.

---

If you are *serious* about becoming a better speaker, then you ought to take Churchill's advice to heart. There were many points along my own public speaking journey where it would have been easier just to quit. If you get to a point in your public speaking journey where you ponder quitting, remind yourself of Winston Churchill's wise words.

## The "Just Give Up Already" Voices

There are other "reasons" why you might be tempted to give up your pursuit of becoming a better speaker—the inner critic's negative messages. Watch out for the little voices that urge you to quit. Some common little voices like that include:

- *I'm so exhausted, I need to stop and give up now.*
- *It's just too much work.*
- *I can't do it.*
- *People give mean feedback. I don't have to put up with that. I'm quitting.*
- *It's too hard.*
- *It doesn't feel like I'm making any progress anyway.*
- *I just want to feel comfortable. I'll be safer if I quit.*
- *I'm not that bad of a speaker.*

- *I'm good enough of a speaker, I can stop now.*

I liken the journey of becoming a better speaker and communicator to a marathon. It's not a sprint that you do once—and that's what you can say in reply to these little voices. Recognize these little voices that urge you to quit and continue to take action anyway.

## It's a Process

As you saw in chapter 6, mastery is a path, it's not a destination. Improvement is a process, and it's an infinite journey.

As you embark on your journey of becoming a better public speaker, it's worth considering the question, "How serious of a student are you?" The room for improvement and growth is the space between your current level of skill all the way to your meeting your full potential.

I love broke-to-billionaire, inspiring teacher, Keith Cunningham's philosophy:

---

## HELL IS MEETING THE PERSON YOU COULD HAVE BEEN.

---

By the same token, hell is meeting the public speaker you could have been.

You've got to put in the work. And it IS work. Again, I'm not going to sugarcoat it for you. You must put the words you've read in this book into action, and you'll be well on your way.

Just remember that Rome wasn't built in a day. And neither was a great public speaker. The process is not a linear path. As you saw in chapter 6, the path more closely resembles an infinity symbol. There is never an end to the pursuit of mastery—and that's a good thing, something to celebrate.

Never lose sight of the big picture.

Remember that the path is as much an inner journey as it is an outer journey, probably more so; hence the reason I titled my approach the "inside-out" approach.

Always remember that whatever you're experiencing, particularly the discouraging moments along the path, that *it's just one step along your journey*. It's never as bad as you think. You never "fail" unless you quit.

Don't be so hard on yourself and remember that you're human.

# CHAPTER 7 GOLDEN NUGGETS

Walking the inside-out approach's path of becoming a better public speaker requires following a process.

It can be a daunting task, no matter your skill level. For that reason, I recommend the inch-by-inch approach and slowly stretching the perimeter of your learning zone—"zoning your zones."

If you're serious about becoming a better speaker, you must commit to staying on the path of learning, meaning you never give up or quit the learning process.

If during your public speaking journey, you feel impatient, remember that it's a process. Like a plant needs time to grow organically, so too do you.

# FINAL THOUGHTS AND PARTING WORDS

As you come to the end of this book, I want to remind you that becoming a better public speaker is not just about working on the mechanics. Working on yourself is equally, if not more, important because you are the common denominator.

You must work on continually empowering yourself and knowing how to get out of your own way when you feel disempowered. Now you have the tools to do so. Now you have the inside-out approach to public speaking.

There is nothing wrong with you.

Although I say that facetiously, I also mean it. As a human being, you tend to feel nervous when speaking in front of a crowd, especially when outside of your comfort zone. You saw that we're hardwired for survival and, therefore, on a constant scan for perceived threats. Our brains command us to perpetually look for what's wrong.

The human need for love and belonging drives our desire for social acceptance. On the flip side of that, this need leads to a huge fear of public judgment and potential social rejection.

We learned that we have an inner critic. What it says to us is the little voice that warns us of danger. It's purpose is to protect us from harm, and it sees public speaking in front of an audience that could potentially reject us as a perceived threat. So what can happen in such a situation if the inner critic is unnoticed or unchecked? We go into survival mode. In essence, our little voices are warning, "If they reject me, I will die!" Again, I say that facetiously, but fear is a primal emotion that gets triggered when we're in a situation that our brain perceives as a threat.

Understanding how the brain and its protection signals work is already half of the battle. Train yourself to monitor and catch what your little voices are saying to you. The antidote to the little voices is awareness and action.

Once you understand this, the only question becomes—what actions should you to take and what continues to drive those actions for the long term? The process of mastery shows us that it's your inner being that ignites the actions necessary to becoming a better speaker.

The desire and hunger to be a better public speaker must come from within you. Get clear on your strongest reasons for walking the path of mastering public speaking. You can enter the path from any skill level. Once you're on it, do the work as prescribed in this book. Put in the work, continually educate yourself, and practice over and over again.

The path is not linear but iterative. There is no destination. There is always another level. And that's a fabulous attribute. Take delight in it.

Create a support team to help encourage you along your journey.

Most importantly, never ever quit. Resist the temptation to quit, no matter how hard it gets at times. Take a breather—literally do breath work!—and *jump back on the horse,* so to speak.

It's been my honor to serve as your guide during the journey of this book.

If you only remember one thing from this whole book, let it be this:

*Be aware of your little voices, catch them as they come up, and take action anyway.*

I believe in you.

With much love and respect,
Mary

# THE "PRESENT" YOURSELF IN PUBLIC SPEAKING COMPANION WORKBOOK

You can download the *"Present" Yourself in Public Speaking Companion Workbook* that contains the worksheets for all of the written exercises in this book at:

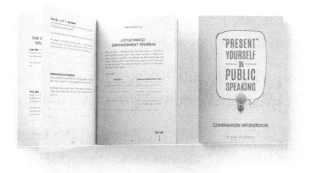

http://magneticpodium.com/pyips-workbook

I highly recommend either using the *"Present" Yourself Companion Workbook* or creating a special journal to have as a place to record your reflections and actions of the written exercises from this book as well as beyond this book as you practice, reflect, and grow in your path to mastery in public speaking and in life.

# MARY'S 2009 WORLD CHAMPIONSHIP SPEECH TRANSCRIPT

**Speech Title: Nelly**

Stop! Reset! Continue . . .

These words made all the difference.

As you can see, I am indeed . . . an Australian . . . trapped in the body of a Chinese.

You see I was born in Hong Kong, and when I was seven years old, my family moved to Australia.

School was tough. I didn't understand the language. Everyone sounded the same [sound effects].

I felt like a fish out of water, like a bird out of its nest, like a guest . . . at a Toastmasters club!

And on this first day of school was when I met her . . . Nelly.

"Just stick with me Mary. No worries, mate!"

Do you remember your childhood best friend? The one who was always with you?

Well, from that day on, Nelly and I were always together. I told her everything, including my frustrations at home. For example, after one semester of school in Australia, I got *six awards:* for running, swimming, music, art, basketball and volleyball.

My mum was so proud . . . I couldn't wait to tell my Dad!

"Dad, Dad! I got six awards, I got six awards!"

[*Pause*]

"Why you not get one for mathematics?"

Dad himself did not get an award for sensitivity.

And when I told Nelly, she said, "Mary, you are bad at math!" A little white lie wouldn't hurt.

Nelly and I went through high school together, we even graduated college.

A few years after college was when reality set in. I had a dead-end job and a dead-end relationship. It's now or never . . . to pursue my childhood dreams . . . of moving to the United State, the land of opportunity!

And when I told Nelly, she said, "You wanna go to New York? You wanna leave this beautiful country? What about your family? What about your friends?"

I thought she was on my side.

As a child she was my friend. As an adult, she was judgmental.

"Mary, you're a fool! If you go, you will fail! Just like you failed your job, just like your relationship, just like mathematics, just like you always fail!"

Do you know what hurt the most?

I believed her!

She kept saying it. "You will fail, you will fail, you will fail!"

"SHUT UPPPP!"

Now you know how Nelly makes me feel . . . let me tell you who she *really* is.

She's not a separate person . . . she's my inner critic.

Do you have an inner critic?

That voice that's always with you, that says "You're not good enough, you're not smart enough, what are people going to think of you?"

What does your inner critic say to you?

And how does it make you feel?

My inner critic . . . my Nelly, was saying, "You will fail!"

Then I remembered my childhood inspiration. A poster of the statue of liberty, representing freedom.

I deserved freedom. Freedom from *Nelly!*

But how do you fight someone that's in your own head?

No matter how many times you punch, and you kick . . . Nelly is still there!

I am *so sick* of Nelly!

And then I read an article that said, "Get out of your head, move forward instead!"

So I contacted the author, and I told him about Nelly . . . and he asked me a very *important* question: "Are you a schizophrenic?"

And then he told me something that changed my life.

He said,"Mary, look, we all have a Nelly. You can't get rid of her. There's no such thing as a *Nelly-ectomy.* Nelly is like a computer program that was created by your past negative experiences. Here's what you can do, I want you to interrupt her immediately by saying: Stop! Reset! Continue . . ."

*Stop*! as in—Whoa, Nelly!

*Reset*! Snap out of it.

And *continue* to take action!"

Stop, Reset, Continue.

Oh! It's like CTRL + ALT + DELETE for Nelly!

So I gave it a try.

"Mary, you don't have what it takes!"

Stop! Reset! Continue!

"You are going to fail!"

Stop! Reset! Continue!

So I packed my bags, moved to the United States, and the Statue of Liberty said, "Welcome to your new life."

Eight years later, I have a career that I love, I am married to my soulmate, I am living my *dream!*

What does your inner critic say to you?

And what are you going to say?

Say it with me!

"Stop! Reset! Continue!"

# ACKNOWLEDGMENTS

There are so many people who have helped me make this book possible:

My accountability partner, Michele Fleury—you rock! You are exactly the right person for me to have travelled this path of authorship with. Thank you for your insights and support. You are truly a kindred spirit. May the world benefit, as I have, from your unique gifts and talents.

My editor, Nancy Pile—to say that you are so much more than an editor would be a gross understatement. You have been a compassionate collaborator who made me feel like I had a friend and cheerleader by my side. Your know-how was invaluable to me. Thank you for "getting me" and helping me pull out what was in my heart and soul, so I could put it onto the page.

My coach, Emily Rose—thank you for helping me stay sane (or semi-sane) during this entire process. Your words and experience were immeasurable.

My designer, Ida Fia Sveningsson—thank you for your amazing talent.

Chandler Bolt—you're the one with the vision that created Self-Publishing School. You are an incredible role model. I consider it serendipitous that I came across you and SPS.

Peggy—thank you for the numerous hours of watching Robbie. Without you this book could not have been written.

And finally, my family, starting with my husband, Rob Cheyne—thank you for your endless support. You are a dream come true to travel this adventure called "life" with. My darling boy, Robbie—you have shown me a depth of love and spirit that I never knew existed. You are my angel and inspiration.

# ABOUT THE AUTHOR

Mary Cheyne (pronounced "sheen"), MBA, was once a self-conscious public speaker and communicator. She has spent the past 15 years learning and mastering effective communication skills.

In 2009, she competed in the World Championship of Public Speaking and out of 25,000 contestants from 14 countries, she placed second. Mary's communications accolades have been featured in *The Boston Globe*, *The World Journal*, as well as TV and radio interviews. She is also the co-author of the book *The Change 8* with Jim Britt, Tony Robbin's first mentor on the topic of conscious communication.

Now Mary is a professional speaker and trainer. She has trained over 15,000 people in over 25 cities around the world and has coached hundreds of individuals on how to become better public speakers and communicators.

As president of Magnetic Podium, LLC, her own training and communications company, she teaches people to communicate clearly both in front of audiences as well as in personal conversations at corporations and organizations. She also teaches communications-related classes at Northeastern University in Boston.

Mary was born in Hong Kong, grew up in Sydney, Australia, and moved to the United States in 2001. She lives in Boston with her husband and three-year-old son.

Find out more at www.MagneticPodium.com

# Urgent Plea!

Thank you for investing in this book!

I really appreciate all of your feedback, and I love hearing what you have to say.

I need your input to make the next version better.

## Please leave me a helpful REVIEW on Amazon

Thank you so much!

*Mary Cheyne*

Made in the USA
Middletown, DE
27 February 2019